Lawrence W.
Lezotte

Jo-Ann Cipriano
Pepperl

The
Effective
Schools
Process:

A Proven
Path to
Learning
for All

Published by:

Effective Schools Products, Ltd.
2199 Jolly Road, Suite 160
Okemos, Michigan 48864
(517) 349-8841 • FAX: (517) 349-8852
http://www.effectiveschools.com

**The Effective Schools Process:
A Proven Path to Learning for All**
Call for quantity discounts.

Book design by Becky Hulburt

Manufactured and printed in the United States of America.

ISBN 1-883247-12-8

Dedicated to the memory of
Ron Edmonds, whose life work continues to
serve as an inspiration to me and educators
everywhere.

Larry Lezotte

*We can, whenever and wherever we choose,
successfully teach all students whose schooling
is of interest to us.*

*We already know more than we need in order to
do that.*

*Whether we do it or not will finally come to
depend on how we feel about the fact that we
haven't done it so far.*

Ron Edmonds

Table of Contents

hapter 1

The Learning Room

My travels as an educational commentator frequently bring me to schools all across our country. One recent episode that typifies the American education system today really stands out in my mind.

I walked into a high school in a town that represents so many in America and noticed an office off to the right of the main entrance. It had a sign above the door that proclaimed "Attendance Office."

Imagine—a whole room was dedicated to the issue of keeping attendance!

With tongue-in-cheek, I asked the principal, "Could you take me to the learning office?"

"We don't have a learning room," he said. "We have an attendance room."

I'm going to make the case that, in your community right now, in the school where you work, in the district where you work, the functional, on-the-ground mission of your school district is compulsory attendance—with learning being optional.

Some of you are going to say, "You're crazy, Larry. We have our mission statement on the wall, on our posters, in our literature, in our correspondence, and everywhere else, and it says we are into the learning mission!"

Let me ask a question then. How often do you formally take attendance? If you're a high school teacher or administrator, you'll probably say that you take attendance every hour of every day. If you're a middle or elementary school teacher, you'll probably say that you take attendance at least every day or every half-day.

Here's my second question. When you take attendance, what do you do? If you're a teacher, you probably put the attendance report outside your door. Somebody from the office comes by and picks it up. The attendance information goes down into the office where it is recorded in the big book. Each school may have a different system or use a different method, but basically that's the procedure.

Once or twice a year, the attendance information is picked up by the central office. The superintendent puts all the attendance data for the district into the trunk of his or her car and drives off to the state department of education.

What does the state department of education give the superintendent in return for these attendance records? Answer: money!

Remember the line in a recent movie: "Show me the money!" Well, follow the money and you'll find the mission. What the money in public education from the states is buying today is attendance. Learning is optional.

Using the same standard of formality, how often do you formally monitor learning?

How often do you put learning reports outside the office?

How often are learning reports picked up and transmitted to the state department of education?

If you do take learning information to the state department of education, what do you get for it? At best, you might get a plaque or a banner to wave at your school. You certainly don't get money for it.

Therein lies the problem. You see, our schools today are not failing under their current mission of compulsory attendance. If you look at the number of kids who drop out of schools, the reading scores of children, and so forth, you'll find that they are more positive than they've ever been in the history of this country. So, to make the argument that schools have failed, and that's why we have to change them, I think falls short of the mark.

The fact of the matter is that, by all data, the system has not failed. Our schools are still delivering to a system that was set up for a different type of society. But, societal changes are quickening at such a pace that the functional mission of our schools—attendance—is no longer sufficient.

What we need to do is to understand at a deeper level why it is that schools are being asked to change. That would give us some clues as to how we have to go about it and what method we have to use.

Chapter 2

The Pace of Change

These three S-curves (waves) illustrate how change is characterized in the United States:

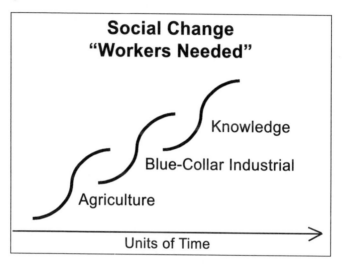

Social Change
"Workers Needed"

Knowledge

Blue-Collar Industrial

Agriculture

Units of Time

Focus on the far left one, where the word "Agriculture" is written. Look at the bottom left of the S-curve. You'll notice that change starts off slowly and then picks up. When it gets out there to the bend, it seems like change has happened virtually overnight! Then it begins to level off.

Here's a great example: if we were to plot people who bought microwave ovens for their homes, you'd find that a few people bought early. Then the pace of buying picked up, until there was a time when it seemed almost everybody was buying microwaves. So, for a time, microwave purchasing blossomed overnight and kept going. Eventually, purchasing started to level off again and then slow down.

This is how change generally operates—slow, fast, overnight explosion, level off, and slow again.

In addition to understanding how change occurs, it's important to realize that our society has gone through two distinct periods in its history, and we're now well into the third. We've gone from agriculture, to blue-collar industrial, and now we're deep into the high-tech/communications/information world—the world where our children are going to have to live and function.

In its prime, the agricultural society required about 95 percent of our citizens to work the land. If they weren't directly working the land, they were one step removed from it. They either grew things, or they helped transport things to market, or they worked to process food.

Now, we have less than five percent of our people working the land. We've gone from 95 percent on the land to 95 percent off the land and, yet, we are still arguably the world's best agricultural producer. This is true, even though we only have five percent of the people working the land.

How did we do this? How did we go from 95 percent on the land to 95 percent off the land, and still maintain our status as number one in the world in terms of agricultural production? The answer is technology!

When technological innovations come along, we are able to displace a lot of workers. So, when 95 percent of America's people began to leave the land, where did they go? They followed the opportunities available to them at the time, and those opportunities were in the growth of the industrial society. That meant many workers had to leave the farm and move to the cities.

When I was growing up near Detroit, it used to be said, only half facetiously, that the social welfare system of the states like Alabama and Louisiana consisted of a bus ticket to Detroit. If people were being displaced off the land because they weren't needed to produce tobacco, rice, cotton, or other crops, what were those states to do with all those displaced workers? We had opportunities in the North—Cleveland, Pittsburgh, Detroit, Chicago, and the places we now refer to as the rust belt—where the heavy industry was. If people could get themselves from where they were to those communities, they could get good-paying jobs and make money to buy homes, cars, and support their families.

When we went from the agricultural wave to the blue-collar industrial wave, we were able to absorb a lot of the displaced farm workers into the blue-collar society. Many of the skills that were required to work the land—a strong back, a good work ethic, a willingness to show up and be there on time— transferred to the factory model. If you had a strong back, a good work ethic, and you could get there on time, you could be making $8, $9, $10, $15, and $20 or more an hour on the line at the automobile factories.

Times are changing again. I have a brother-in-law who works at a Mazda plant near Detroit. He's a factory worker, in that sense, but his major responsibility is to service robots. The skills that he needs to do the job that he has been hired to do are very technical skills. This is happening throughout our nation, in just about every industry, as people move out of the blue-collar industrial society and into the high-tech/communications/information society. The new skills require computer knowledge, communications knowledge, and more.

What we have now is this whole new displacement of workers. Jobs are being eliminated in the old blue-collar industrial factory or are changing to require more technical skills. As we move into this knowledge-worker world, this has major ramifications for what it is that people need to know and be able to do in order to fit into this new society and be able to add value to their industries.

This is a vision of where we are today in the United States, between the skill levels that the schools are producing and the skill levels that are needed in society:

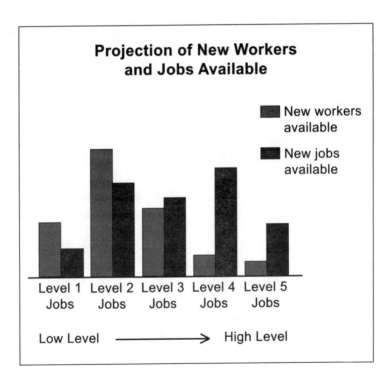

Level 1 jobs are low-skill jobs, while Level 5 jobs require very sophisticated skills and training. Here's a listing of these types of jobs and their requirements:

Projection of New Workers and Jobs Available

Level 1 Jobs:
- Limited vocabulary of 2,500 words
- Read 125 words/minute
- Write simple sentences

Unskilled manual laborer	Fast food worker

Level 2 Jobs:
- Reading vocabulary of 5,000 words
- Read 195–215 words/minute
- Write compound sentences

Old-style assembly line	Assembler
Machine operator	Truck driver

Level 3 Jobs:
- Read safety rules and equipment instructions
- Write simple reports

Retail sales	Mechanic	Order clerk
Secretary	New-style work teams	Telephone repair

Level 4 Jobs:
- Read journals and manuals
- Write business letters and reports

Nurse	Middle-management
Teacher	Technician

Level 5 Jobs:
- Read scientific/technical journals and financial reports
- Write speeches and articles

Researcher	Engineer	Professor
Doctor	Architect	Lawyer

For the most part, the profile of high school graduates in America fits the skill levels needed for Level 2 jobs. The next most frequent level of skills high school graduates possess fit Level 3 jobs and Level 1 jobs. Notice that there are few young people coming out with skills for Level 4 and 5 jobs.

On the demand side, or what jobs are available in society, the most opportunities are in Levels 3, 4, and 5. In fact, there are more jobs available than we have people trained to fill them. On Levels 1 and 2, though, we have more people with low skills than the jobs to absorb them.

This represents a huge supply-and-demand discrepancy. The schools, and what they are doing, are not aligning with the need to prepare people to live, function, and work in this new high-tech/communications/information society. This, in a nutshell, is what's propelling and compelling school reform.

Here's one definition of insanity: the belief that, if we do again what we've been doing, we're going to get different results.

Obviously, if we do again what we've been doing, we're going to get again what we've been getting—over and over. Is that what we want and need?

Schools are still preparing people for the blue-collar industrial world, but that world is rapidly changing. Certainly, our schools are not failing by yesterday's measures, but they simply are not doing what they need to do by tomorrow's measures.

Chapter 3

Compulsory Learning

Each time society changes, we have a change in the mission of public education. In the early period of the agrarian society, only the very wealthy (those who could get the work done on the land by hiring others) could afford the luxury of sending their own children off for formal schooling. The mission during much of the agrarian society was schooling for some, an elite kind of concept.

In one of the biographies of Alex Haley, his great-grandmother says to his great-grandfather, "Look, we have eight children. Can't we waste one?"

Her idea of "wasting one" was to have one formally educated, and this is what she was pushing for on behalf of her son, Alex Haley's grandfather. When you had a large family in an agricultural society, your productivity as a family unit went up because you had more children to work the land. To have a child leave the land to go off somewhere for formal schooling was considered a waste of good labor. How times have changed over the last 100 to 150 years!

When we started leaving the agrarian society and going into the blue-collar industrial society, Horace Mann, the commissioner of education in the Commonwealth of Massachusetts, became the principal advocate and architect for the common school movement in this country. He proposed a system that would allow all children of our nation to have access to basic school skills.

When Horace Mann went into the political arena to make the case for the common school, the vision for productivity, efficiency, and effectiveness spreading across the land was the vision of the factory. Basically, what Horace Mann said to the political leaders of his commonwealth was, "Look, if you give us enough money to create a system of public schools that will allow all of the children to be educated, the schools can and will look a lot like factories."

People believed that you could bring kids in and "batch process" them just like you would if you were making shoes, cars, or any other product. They could be processed down the line, as it were, and then graduated at the end of the line with the necessary knowledge and skills.

Horace Mann knew from day one that we would have fatalities in this kind of one-size-fits-all factory model. The system was never designed to be successful for all children. He knew, however, that, in the industrial society, we didn't need to have all the children educated! Remember, there were low-skill jobs for some and modest-skill jobs for others. While we needed strong leaders to provide the overall guidance for our factory model, the schools could afford not to have success for all kids.

As we go into the high-tech/communications/information society, we have to shift the mission again. When Horace Mann gave us the common school, the functional mission of public education that he left us with was the mission of compulsory attendance with learning being optional. This mission fulfilled the needs of the industrial society.

As we progress through the high-tech/communications/information society, though, we can no longer afford this. The new mission of public education must change. The new mission of public education must be compulsory learning. It's going to require a whole different mind-set.

You've probably heard the notion that "form ought to follow function." What we have in public education is a form of schooling designed to deliver the function of compulsory attendance with learning being optional.

To change the function of a system, you also have to change the form. If you try to deliver a new function in an old form, the old form will reclaim the function. If you try to convey a compulsory learning mission in a system that was designed first for compulsory attendance, with learning being optional, you're not going to be very successful for very long.

We have to begin to change the system and change the form, and the first step in doing that is to change the mission. The new mission for the 21st century school district is the mission of **Learning for All: Whatever it Takes!**

New Mission

Learning For All—

WHATEVER IT TAKES!

Let's imagine you're a field general and you have an army at your disposal. I'll pretend I'm the supreme allied commander (and that's a real stretch). I'll call you and all of your fellow field generals into the war room.

"Ladies and gentlemen," I'll say, "I, as your supreme allied commander, want to tell you ahead of time that at noon Eastern Standard Time today, we are going to declare war!"

Since you are in command of the troops that have to "fight" in this war, I want to be very sure that you understand the mission. "Quite clearly, the mission is **Learning for All: Whatever it Takes**," I'll bellow. "Now, are there any questions?"

Some of you might raise your hands and say, "Dear, supreme allied commander, sir (I'm loving this), could you say a little bit more about what you mean by all?"

"Well, all means all," I'll say.

"Does this include disadvantaged kids who come to our schools?"

"All equals all."

"Does all mean inclusive of the special-needs kids?"

"All means all."

"You mean to tell me that the new mission of public education not only includes the special-education children, but also those low-incidence special category kids, the severely and profoundly handicapped kids?"

"The bottom line is, all equals all."

You'll think about that for a minute and probably say, "Wow! This is not going to be an easy war to win!"

I would remind you that a mission statement is not supposed to be a description of current reality. A mission statement is supposed to be a description of a preferred future. **Learning for All: Whatever it Takes** is a description of a preferred future for this country.

Now having clarified the mission, one of you is likely to raise your hand and say, "O.K., dear supreme allied commander, now that I know what all means, the next question that comes to mind is, learn what? What is it that we want kids to learn under this new mission of **Learning for All**?"

The definition of learning that you are expected to respond to is a definition that has to be put into the context of your state. This comes from the fact that, in our Constitution, the first responsibility for defining the aims and ends of public education are vested in each of the individual states. Theoretically, we could have 50 different definitions. My home state of Michigan's definition of core learning for its children under this new mission of **Learning for All** might look a bit different than it would for New York, Colorado, or California.

The first phone call you have to make, if you will, is to your own state department to ask the people there what it is the state wants the kids to know, do, and be disposed to do when they finish their time in the public school system. Almost all of the 50 states, to my knowledge, have defined—at least in core terms—what it is they want their kids to know, do, and be disposed to do. In Michigan, it's called the core curriculum. Other states call it essential student learnings, desired learning performances, essential curriculum, or whatever. Each state has a responsibility and the authority to define initially the aims and end of public education.

Districts have authority to do things beyond the minimums defined by the state, but they do not have the authority to ignore state requirements. Your local district has the authority to set expectations for learning that are above and beyond your state's expectations. The local district must be able to demonstrate that what it wants the kids to know and do is inclusive of what the state requires.

Likewise, following this conceptualization, individual schools could have a bigger circle of expectations for essential learnings, even beyond the district and the state. However, the school's expectations must be inclusive of both what the state says it wants and what the district says it wants.

Even going beyond that, individual teachers, in their own content or subject matter or grade level areas, can have expectations of learning for their students that are above the schools. But, again, they have to be able to demonstrate that, if the kids learn what they're being taught in that teacher's classroom, they will be able to meet the standards set by the building, the district, and the state.

Parents and individual students may set goals for themselves that go beyond the requirements of the teacher, and that's wonderful, as far as I'm concerned. There is nothing in this formulation of defining learning in a political and legal way that has to put a cap on what kids learn. What it does is set some perimeters, standards, and benchmarks. Each of those levels and layers in the system has the authority to do what I just described and, not only do they have the authority, it seems to me they have the obligation to do this.

I don't believe that any student ought to have to take a seat in any classroom in America unless the teacher in that classroom can make it clear what results, outcomes, performance, and achievements are expected of that child.

I don't think any teacher ought to have to take up a teaching station in any classroom in America unless the principal of that school can make it clear what results are expected of that teacher.

I don't think any principal ought to have to take up a post anywhere in America unless the superintendent, operating as an agent of the board and as an agent of the state, can make it clear to that principal what results are expected from the school.

I think the superintendent and local board have a right to expect the state to define the essential core learnings.

I have defined learning in terms of the individual student, teacher, school, district, and state requirements. I have defined all as literally everyone. The third piece of the mission statement is **Whatever it Takes**. You never commit troops to a mission unless you've made the rules of engagement clear. What will teachers be permitted to do, and prohibited from doing, pursuant to the **Learning for All** mission?

The federal government and, earlier on, some of the states, tried to write the rules of engagement. For example, zero tolerance rules say you cannot bring any kind of drug on campus. If you're caught with a substance on campus, you will be expelled or suspended for some period of time. This was all with the best of intent, but because we didn't clarify the rules and tried to write those rules from afar, we ended up with cases like a girl being thrown out of high school for having aspirin in her purse or locker. We had people being thrown out because they ostensibly brought a butter knife to campus to use at lunch and it's being called a weapon.

We're trying, with the best of intentions, to write these rules of engagement, but the further you try to write those rules from the point of service delivery on the shop floor of the school classroom, the more difficult it is to write rules that are going to be sensible.

I believe each school and district must talk about what they will be permitted to do and prohibited from doing pursuant to the **Learning for All** mission. Writing the rules of engagement together, making sure they make sense for your situation, and agreeing upon them are critical steps in reaching the new mission.

hapter 4

Basic Beliefs

There are several basic beliefs or assumptions that are the underpinning of the **Learning for All** mission. If you've heard me speak or read my book, *Learning for All*, these will look familiar to you, but I'd like to explore them further and add a few that you may not have considered before.

In fact, I'd like to suggest that each teacher in your school respond to each of these beliefs. Set up a Likert scale from strongly agree to strongly disagree, and see where your teachers fall.

All children can learn and come to school motivated to do so.

O	O	O	O	O
Strongly Agree	Agree	Undecided	Disagree	Strongly Disagree

Mrs. Jones, who teaches second grade, might say to me, "Well, this is mostly true, but you haven't met Jimmy in my class."

We've got a problem. We've got a basic fundamental belief that we have to buy into in order to forward the new mission—all children can learn and come to school motivated to do so. However, Mrs. Jones just told me that's not true for Jimmy. Now what are we going to do?

W. Edwards Deming, the quality guru, said that one of the first and foremost things you do in creating a quality system is to create consistency of purpose for the improvement of products and the system. We cannot let Mrs. Jones' statement that Jimmy is unable to learn stand, because it will undermine the consistency of purpose. We can't threaten her out of it, so we're painting ourselves into a corner.

Or are we? I could ask Mrs. Jones, "Can Jimmy walk?"

She'll tell me, "Yes, of course, he can."

That would allow us to believe that Jimmy was motivated to learn at about age one or one-and-a-half to walk. If, by the way, you need any renewal of the spirit about the educability of all children, go out and find yourself a toddler who is learning to walk right now. They pull themselves up by the table, chair, davenport, or whatever, and they muster up enough courage to let go. Maybe they fall down and bump their arm, but they get up and do it again. If the human spirit doesn't come hard-wired with a deep yearning for learning, please explain this to me: why would a child who does something and does not succeed and, in fact, may get hurt for a moment, ultimately get up and do it again time after time? There is a deep motivation for learning!

The next question I'd ask Mrs. Jones is, "Can Jimmy talk?"

"Yes, that's part of the problem," she'll say. "He talks all the time!"

That says to me that Jimmy was motivated at about age two or two-and-a-half to learn to talk. That's when kids begin to pick up vocabulary and learn phrases.

"Can Jimmy follow commands?" I'll ask.

"If I say, Jimmy, sit down, he will sit for a minute," Mrs. Jones might tell me, "but then he's up wandering around again."

Where am I going with all of these questions? I want Mrs. Jones to come to this conclusion: Jimmy is not motivated to learn what it is that she wants him to learn in the way she wants him to learn it at this time.

If I can get Mrs. Jones to come to that conclusion, I've done some very important things. Number one, I've maintained consistency of purpose around the issue that all children can learn if motivated to do so.

Number two, I've just given Mrs. Jones hope. Maybe, for Jimmy, the reform is around the **when**. Maybe, for Jimmy, the reform is around the **how**. Maybe, for Jimmy, the reform is around the **what**. These three possibilities give our teacher hope, but also make it clear that the core belief of **Learning for All** still stands.

The individual school controls enough variables to assure that all children do learn.

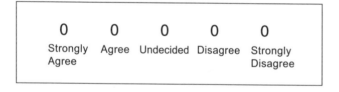

This belief is actually harder for more teachers to embrace than the first one. Most teachers will tell me, "I believe that all children can learn. I just don't believe that I have control over enough of the variables to assure that they do."

I'll frequently ask educators across the country, "What one variable do you feel that you do not control at your school, but if you did, it would make all the difference in student learning?"

The most frequent answer I get back is "the parents."

Teachers and administrators tell me, "We don't and can't control the parents, and they're part of the problem."

The children who go to your school come from one of three types of families. First, there are parents who, by your definition, are doing everything that parents should do on the home side to assure high levels of success in school. In other words, they're already doing it right.

What should the school's response to these parents be? I would argue that the school's response should be to nurture them, encourage them, and strengthen their good influence as time goes on.

The second group of parents is not now doing what they ought to do on the home side to assure high levels of success in school, but the reason is grounded in ignorance. That sounds like a harsh statement, but think about it this way: in the United States, we license and certify everything and anything, except what? There's no requirement to be a parent! The safest assumption one can make about parenting skills and competency is to make no assumption.

If parents are not doing the right thing at home and it's grounded in ignorance, how should the schools respond to those parents? Develop an outreach program to begin to work with your parents to help them learn to do the kinds of things they should do to help nurture success in school for their children. There are many successful examples out there.

The third kind of parents, the toughest group of all from a moral point of view, are parents who, even if they knew better, wouldn't do anything to help their children in school. What should the school's response be in this sad case?

It seems to me the school's moral obligation ought to be to try to develop an in-school capability to connect with those kids in a way that stimulates or nurtures the home/school experience inside the school.

A school's stakeholders are the most qualified people to implement the needed changes.

Who makes up the stakeholders to a school? The internal stakeholders are obvious—the teachers, support staff, administrators, and all of the people who work inside the school.

The external stakeholders would include those people on the outside who can and do play an important role in sharing in the school's success. The obvious group would be parents, but we must also include the political leaders in our community, religious leaders, business leaders, and all other external stakeholder groups whose taxes help support schools.

As a matter of fact, the changing demographics in many communities means that only a relatively small percent of the people in the community have children in the schools. We need to find ways of engaging segments of the nonparent population in school reform.

In some of the places where we're losing the reform initiative, we're losing it not so much from resistance inside the schools, but from resistance from one segment or another of the external stakeholder groups.

You and your colleagues are already doing the best you know to do, given the conditions in which you find yourselves.

0	0	0	0	0
Strongly Agree	Agree	Undecided	Disagree	Strongly Disagree

The implications are twofold. Since you and your colleagues are already doing the best you know to do, given the conditions, if you want to change the outcomes, you've got to get new knowledge into the system.

You also need to change the conditions. If you try to change the knowledge states, without changing the conditions, you're going to end up with very frustrated teachers! More often than not, if you try to put new knowledge into an old condition or old system, the system will win out. Most workers, in any organization, cannot go to work day after day and swim upstream against the whitewater of the system. People tire; people wear down.

When we start trying to push new knowledge in, but don't change the conditions, we're going to get in trouble. On the other side, you can't change the conditions without, at the same time, changing the knowledge states of your people. If you try to do that, you're going to end up with change without difference. We have to be prepared, then, as a part of our overall strategy to change the knowledge states of our people and, at the same time, tether that new knowledge together with changes in the condition.

School by school change is the best hope for reforming the schools.

O	O	O	O	O
Strongly Agree	Agree	Undecided	Disagree	Strongly Disagree

Each school is different with different needs, strengths, and weaknesses. Each school is going to be able to move at different rates. We're going to have to customize this to the school level. The centerpiece of our reform package is one of building, developing, implementing, and sustaining reform, school by school, one school at a time.

At the end of the day, the model that we're going to put in place will have to allow each individual campus to develop off of its own strengths, own needs, and own plan, to move forward on the **Learning for All** mission.

In America, economic development, community development, and educational development are woven together like the strands of a rope. If we have large numbers of kids leaving our schools without the necessary knowledge, skills, attitudes, and dispositions to go into the world of work and into society in general and contribute in a positive way, then our ability, as a nation, to succeed and compete in the international market is going to be significantly and substantially impaired.

School reform is not only worth doing and must be done, it's a manageable task that can be done.

There are only two kinds of schools in the United States—improving schools and declining schools.

0	0	0	0	0
Strongly Agree	Agree	Undecided	Disagree	Strongly Disagree

You may say, "Now, wait a minute! I think our school may not be improving as much as we'd like or maybe not at all, but we're surely not declining!"

Because of the changing context of our society— the high-tech / communications / information world, the international global economy, and all that is implied in those kinds of terms—it seems to me that, if a school isn't improving, it's declining! If it sees itself more or less as a status quo school, then status quo has to be placed in the category of decline. You're either improving or declining.

Once we accept that belief, most of us would want to affiliate ourselves with an improving effort. (I doubt anyone would want to be part of a declining effort.)

I suggest the principal take a sheet of paper, fold it in half, and make two columns. At the head of one column, write, *"We, the undersigned, would like to be part of an improving school."*

On the other column, write, *"We, the undersigned, would like to be part of a declining school."*

Ask the staff to weigh in on it and see where people come out.

You can anticipate there are going to be some in the school who will ask, "What are the hidden implications of this two-column sign-up sheet?"

There are no hidden implications! There are simply two choices. As a school, we can either choose to pursue the notion of improving or we can choose to pursue the notion of decline—but we can't stay still, and that's the issue I'm trying to force out on the table.

Every school can improve.

0	0	0	0	0
Strongly Agree	Agree	Undecided	Disagree	Strongly Disagree

There is no such thing as the perfect school. The common element across all schools in America is that every school can improve; however, what constitutes improvement and what constitutes each increment of improvement should be put in the context of each school, school by school.

That's what makes the model of the effective schools process so powerful! It acknowledges that you have to couple up your initiatives with where you are. You start with your strengths and your needs, and move from there. The strengths and needs in any given school may be different from the school down the street.

The needed capacity to improve your school resides in your school right now.

0	0	0	0	0
Strongly Agree	Agree	Undecided	Disagree	Strongly Disagree

There are many educators who have come to believe that, if they're going to make significant changes in the achievement levels of the children who attend their school, it's going to require an infusion of new people, new programs, new resources, or something from the outside. This belief states that you already have within you the wherewithal to make significant differences—without a significant infusion of new people, new programs, or new resources.

I know a lot of people don't believe this. I've often heard educators say, "We've gone as far as we can until we get those extra resources or people" or whatever.

Bring the teachers and administrators together in your school and create a dialogue around the mission of **Learning for All**. Begin to ask questions like, "What are the current barriers to continuous improvement on the **Learning for All** mission? What are some ideas that we can come up with that will make our school better?"

I guarantee you, if you let that dialogue play itself out, and then take action where there is some degree of consensus, you will be surprised at the level of improvement that can be realized without all of the extras on the outside.

It may sound funny to hear this coming from me— an outside consultant on effective schools—but, in fact, you don't even need me! There may be a role for somebody like me to come into your school and quickly get you and your faculty thinking and talking about ideas that will connect for your situation and your school, but the capacity to do the changing and to make the school a better place resides in your school right now.

All of the adults in the school are important.

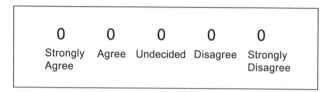

There's nobody more important in a school than the teachers in terms of meeting the learning goals of the kids. But you have to understand the school culture or climate is carried on the back of all of the adults in the school—cooks, custodians, bus drivers, school secretaries, administrators, and guidance counselors, as well as teachers and others.

One of the questions my friend and former colleague at Michigan State University, Dr. Wilbur Brookover, researched was, "If I could only be at your school for an hour, and my goal in coming was to try to get as rich of a description as I could of the climate of the school, where would you have me spend that hour? Would you have me spend it going from classroom to classroom? Would you have me spend it out in the hall, in the cafeteria, talking to the principal, calling parents, interviewing students? What would you have me do?"

What Brookover's research found was, if you only have an hour to capture the climate of the school, the place to spend that hour would be within sight and earshot of the school secretary. Every significant human interaction within the school occurs proximate to the school secretary.

If you want to know how the big people of the school relate to the little people, watch how the school secretary relates to the little girl who comes in off the playground with a scuffed knee.

If you want to know how the big people in the school relate to other big people, watch how the school secretary interacts with the teachers as they come in and out of the office area.

If you want to know how the school feels about the parents of the kids who go there, watch how the school secretary answers the telephone.

If you want to know how authority structures work in the school, watch where the school secretary positions herself physically, as well as organizationally, in relation to the principal.

I was talking about these beliefs at a conference once, when a principal came up to me at the break. He said, "You know, I kind of resented it when you told me the school secretary was so important. I always thought I was as important as anybody in my school because you talk so much about instructional leadership. But I thought about it some more and I have to conclude you're right. Let me give you an example. Last year, on Valentine's Day, I received four Valentines from the faculty. The school secretary got 37! I think I know where the values are!"

I'm not trying to make hierarchical statements. That's not the important issue. I'm trying to illustrate that, as a very important contributor to school climate, if you're going to try to make changes in your school that will matter, you want to include the school secretary as part of the discourse. All adults are important in the school.

Change is a process, not an event.

0	0	0	0	0
Strongly Agree	Agree	Undecided	Disagree	Strongly Disagree

I would retire tomorrow and be a rich person if I had all the money that's going to be spent in the United States in one school year chasing school reform as if it were an event.

Attending a conference or having a speaker in is an event. I'm not discouraging this, but events don't change schools. Long-term ongoing processes change schools.

What am I suggesting? If you are going to sponsor teachers to go off to a state math conference or a national meeting on effective schools or any myriad of possibilities out there, make sure there is some lead-up to it. There should be processes going on in the school that make it clear why teachers are going to that event. When they return, they should not just come back feeling good about going and then conduct business as usual. A process should be in place whereby teachers come back and plug into an ongoing dialogue that does something with what they've learned. We want a lead-up to the event, then the event itself, and the discussion and implementation to follow it.

Existing people are the best change agents.

0	0	0	0	0
Strongly Agree	Agree	Undecided	Disagree	Strongly Disagree

These people may need to learn new things and to do different things, but they are the best change agents. In order for change to succeed, it must come from the inside. You've got to believe that the existing people are the best change agents. It's not somebody else. It's not from somewhere down the street. It's us—here and now.

The beliefs outlined in this chapter must be present to prepare the school for change or create a culture that is receptive to change.

Chapter 5

A Shift in System

Changing the mission of public education from compulsory attendance with optional learning to compulsory learning represents a significant paradigm shift. Most would argue that the paradigm shift is at least equal in magnitude to the shift that occurred when we, as a nation, went from optional schooling to compulsory schooling with optional learning.

Sometimes people find it easier to see the significance of a change like this if they can see it first in another field. For example, like public education, health care and the medical model are undergoing a major paradigm shift. Most would agree that the U.S. health care system is one of the best in the world. The dominant approach of the physician in the United States has been to treat the patient's illness. Why does it need to change?

It needs to change because we've learned more—more about preventing illness, more about keeping healthy, and more about taking an active role in our own health care. The emerging health and wellness paradigm shifts the mind-set from treating an illness to healing the body. The difference is that treating an illness is always outside in. Healing the body is always inside out. The role of the health-care-giver changes from being in charge of treatment to being more of a partner in healing. Those in medicine will probably find this shift in mind-set terribly difficult to internalize.

In many ways, the emerging health care model parallels the changes experienced by educators as we go from the mission of compulsory attendance with optional learning to compulsory learning. Teaching, like treating, is always outside in. Learning, like healing, is always inside out.

Educators are going to have to change from telling the learners what to do and how to do it, toward becoming a partner in learning with the student. This represents a major shift in thinking. "Telling is not teaching" and "listening is not learning" take on added significance in this context.

Will public school districts successfully meet the challenge of change or are they likely to disappear, as many have predicted and some have even hoped? Of course, you might point out that school district structures have been part of the public education system from the beginning. Why is there even a question about their survival, and why should they change at all?

I can give you six reasons right off the bat:

1 Organizations in every type of industry are eliminating layers and layers of bureaucratic structures, in part to help contain costs and eliminate redundancy, thus moving decision-making as close to the point of service delivery as possible. School districts represent a layer between the state and the school.

2 Whole countries, like New Zealand, have eliminated their equivalent of the local school district. Instead, school governance has been moved to the individual schools.

3 Whole states, like Kentucky and Texas, have essentially mandated site-based management and created school-level governance mechanisms.

4 Examples of good practice in private and parochial schools, for the most part, do not exist in a district context.

5 Charter schools in many states have school-level governance, but do not exist as part of a school district and they seem able to do just fine.

6 Charter schools and schools managed by "for profit" companies are willing to offer programs that sometimes include a personal computer for every child and virtually guarantee results. Most public school districts are unable or unwilling to compete.

For these reasons and more, I say that the chances the local school district will survive are no better than 50/50. Districts may disappear even as their individual schools survive.

Proponents of the district model usually argue that districts are most cost-effective and efficient when it comes to such things as purchasing, transportation, food services, and the like. If this argument is true, why are so many districts outsourcing and privatizing these very services? If you guessed to save money, you get to go to the head of the class!

Proponents of the district model might argue that district-level governance increases the articulation and vertical integration of services. If this argument is true, why do so many school districts fail the test of alignment between curriculum, instruction, and assessment? And, why are so many districts moving toward site-based management?

Proponents of the district model say that district-level governance provides assurance that qualified candidates are hired for different positions in the schools. If this argument is true, why do so many principals long for a time when they can hire their own staff members and not be forced to take those sent over to the school from the central office?

Proponents of the district model point out that the district organization increases accountability. If this argument is true, why are the individual states shifting their accountability systems to the school level?

People who work in the marketing field often have the problem of deciding when to stop marketing a particular product. One test they impose on themselves is to ask the question, "Knowing what we know now, if we weren't already marketing this product, would we start?"

If the answer is "no," then the decision is made to stop marketing the product.

Let's use that question in the case of school districts. Knowing what we know now, if we didn't already have local school districts in place, would we create them—especially if the governance already existed at the school level?

I don't believe we would. The main argument favoring the survival of the district-level governance model is that we already have it—it enjoys the status of the incumbent—not because it works so well.

Education is clearly a growth industry. If shares were being traded on the New York Stock Exchange, I'd tell you to buy as many as you could. However, I'd be a lot more conservative regarding advising you to invest in public schools as the major institution to deliver the expanded educational mission.

How can you have an expanding market and such a pessimistic view about the main institution delivering to that market? Let me give you an example that illustrates how you can have such a situation. Catalog sales have been a real growth industry in the United States. Chances are, on any given day, when you come home from work, you'll find two, three, or more catalogs in your mailbox. The amount of money people spend buying things through catalogs has gone up steadily in the last 10 years.

In spite of this massive growth, one company— once the very leader in catalog sales—ended its catalog business. The Sears catalog went out of business in 1993, right in the midst of an expanding market. Fifteen years earlier, Sears had an 85 percent market share in catalog sales. They basically owned the market. They had as much market share in catalog sales as public schools do today in the education business.

Catalog sales were on the upswing, but the Sears catalog went out of business. Why? Sears could not manage change. They could not change their organizational structure enough to keep up with the pace of changing conditions and new competitors. The new kids on the block were able to adapt where the once giant leader was not. There is certainly no guarantee that the people who own the market can survive the changes needed to continue to grow and thrive.

W. Edwards Deming points out that it's virtually impossible to change a system from the inside. Think about the implications of this statement. If you work for a district or a school, if you're a teacher or an administrator, you're clearly an insider trying to think about how you can lead and participate in a meaningful way in the change process. Then a person like Deming comes along and says it's virtually impossible to change the system from within the system. That would suggest that you may as well give up, go home, and wait until the end comes!

But Deming goes on to say more. He tells us, if we're going to try to change a system from inside, we need to do two things:

The people who are inside the system need to behave, part of the time, as if they were outside the system. You have to go up on he hill and get a different vantage point.

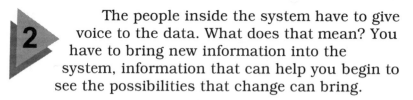

The people inside the system have to give voice to the data. What does that mean? You have to bring new information into the system, information that can help you begin to see the possibilities that change can bring.

My friend and author, Patrick Dolan, in one of his books on restructuring schools, has this great line that I love: "Since the second day of creation, all change has had to work against a system-in-place."

Don't ever underestimate the power of the system already there to want to sustain itself! Look at this graph of the western organizational model:

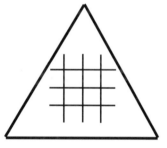

The System-in-Place

All Change Occurs Against the System-in-Place

It's a pyramid to signify that the top of the system is where the command and control centers (and the authority) of the organization reside. The bottom of the pyramid is where the accountability and responsibility live.

Any time an organization separates authority on one end, from accountability and responsibility on the other, as we typically do in our organizational pattern in the United States, the makings of a dysfunctional system exist!

Notice on the inside of the pyramid are horizontal lines meant to signify the layers in the system. The system of public education in the United States is a deeply layered one. Students are layered in classrooms; classrooms are layered inside school buildings; school buildings are layered into districts; and districts are layered into states.

If the people at the top want to ask for change—or even require or mandate it—they will have to be able to send the message in a strong enough way to penetrate all the way down to the bottom of the organization.

The graph also has vertical lines to signify the silos inside the system. The system of public education has several silos associated with it. We might have the regular education silo, the special education silo, the gifted and talented silo, and so on. Typically, people inside a silo only talk to each other. The special-ed people at the school level talk to the special-ed people at the district level who communicate with the special-ed people at the state level.

When you create a highly top-down system like this—where the control and authority is at the top, the accountability is at the bottom, and it's deeply layered and vertically siloed—there is an enormous amount of inertia to do again tomorrow what it did yesterday. You can walk away from a system like this for 1,000 years and it will continue to be doing what it was doing when you left. That is its strength, and that's wonderful if the system is doing what you want it to do. But that same strength becomes its greatest liability when you want change.

If you want the system to do something differently tomorrow than what it did yesterday, you're going to have a problem! One of the reasons is it's virtually impossible to get good information back from the bottom of the system to the top, regarding how well the system is working.

Business leaders, community leaders, and political leaders are putting pressure on schools and on the state departments, saying, "We want accountability!"

The state departments are yelling down to the individual schools, asking, "How's it going out there?"

The schools, at the bottom of the system, are saying, "It's going great. Just leave us alone. Send a little more money."

The people at the bottom of the system, the frontline workers, the teachers and others who are out there on the frontlines of education everyday, have long since realized that the people at the top of the system do not want to hear bad news. Also, even if the people at the bottom of the system have enough courage to be willing to express bad news, they realize from past experience that, if you start sending bad news up through the inside of a deeply layered system, by the time it gets to the top, it will be turned into good news anyway. Or, odds are, you'll be punished for being a whistle-blower. For these reasons, people down on the bottom aren't likely to freely tell the truth.

So how do states, under pressure to hold schools accountable and unable to get information from inside the system, handle this? They've developed statewide testing programs. I use a metaphor of a train to describe the process. Once a year, the train goes out around the system, to the classrooms of schools across the state. The train picks up a reading score here and a math score there, and brings it back to the top (the state). The state then reports the information out, and that's supposed to stand as accountability inside the system.

When I speak to groups of teachers, I'll frequently ask them to raise their hands as a "yes" sign to my question, "How many of you believe that the assessment system of your state represents a fair and just measure of your work as a school and as a teacher?"

Virtually no hands go up.

Then I'll address principals. "How many of you believe that the assessment system of your state adds up to a fair and just measure of your work as a principal?"

Again, no hands go up.

You can't develop an accountability system with information from inside the system, so you develop one by going around the system, as most of the current assessment programs do. You may get a score, but nobody feels it's a fair and just measure of his or her work. How many times have you heard the argument, "We ought not to be so concerned with test scores?" Those inside the system try to disown the scores.

If I could talk to the legislators and governors of most states and get them to listen, I think I could get them to understand that there are decided limits to what you can do if you try to use a top-down system to collect information as we have been trying to do. You've got to build a capacity into the organizational model so the people at the bottom of the system not only feel accountable and responsible, but also feel a sense of commitment to the system. If they have a commitment to the accountability system, they feel some sense of authority and ownership in it.

When somebody wants to run for President of the United States, one of the things he or she routinely does as part of the effort to get the nomination, whether Democrat or Republican, is make trips to foreign countries to get an up-close-and-personal feel for what power relationships look like in Bosnia, the Middle East, and other trouble spots we have to contend with in the world. Why not have that same expectation for elected officials who are going to take action in education? Why not insist that they go to the frontlines, up close and personal?

Most of the states I have worked in have required their schools and districts to develop a comprehensive technology plan. They're making demands that the schools do this and that to fulfill the technology goal. The fact of the matter is probably 90 percent of the schools in America do not even have the electrical outlets to have enough computers in all classrooms. They're given money to get kids on the Internet and they don't have the phone lines to make the connections. Our elected officials have a vision of the system that is not at all accurate. If they would spend a little time there before they take action. I think in many cases they would back up and go about things in a different way.

Are there some alternative formulations out there? Yes! One of them has been suggested by Sally Helgesen, the author of *The Female Advantage* and *The Web of Inclusion*. She discovered that organizations that are really successful and profitable in their lines of endeavor, whether run by men or women, do not fit into the organizational model of the pyramid. Instead, the organizational model that works the best actually looks something like a spider web.

If you've ever looked at a spider web, you know it's flat, flexible, and strong. The center of the web is as dependent on the outside as the outside is on the center. It's a very different model from the top-down pyramid.

Chapter 6

Pulling in the Anchors

We have an entrenched history in schools of the top-down pyramid model, deeply layered and deeply siloed, with an enormous amount of inertia to do again what it's always done. If we want to change schools, we have to acknowledge this system-in-place and be prepared to take it on. How do we begin to change such a system?

Author Pat Dolan gives us some answers. He says that a system is held in place by a set of anchors. Think about a lawn tent. Let's say you're going to have a wedding reception outside and you want to protect your guests from the rain or sun. What is it that holds that tent in place? Obviously, it's the anchoring lines that come off the sides.

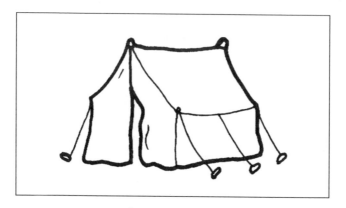

What if you wanted to relocate that tent to a different, more aesthetically appealing side of your yard with a nice view of the garden? Where would you start the process? You'd start by dealing with the anchors.

When we talk about changing the system called public education in your state, your district, and your school, we have to start by acknowledging that we have anchors-in-place. We have to start our negotiation, if you will, with these anchors.

The first anchor to the system-in-place is the school board. The board, with the authority to make decisions and set local policy, represents one of the major anchors.

Teachers and administrators oftentimes say the problem with their school district is the school board. At one level, I know some of this complaining helps them rationalize conditions. Blaming someone else feels good and it's a tempting thing to do. Blame it on the board! On another level, though, my experience has shown that boards could very well be a bigger part of the problem than most are willing to admit.

One of the most profound examples I can come up with happened in the Province of New Brunswick, Canada. I was there one summer with some colleagues, talking about school reform. The Canadian Prime Minister had received authority from Parliament to eliminate all local elected school boards—and did just that. The superintendent was established as a civil servant reporting directly to the Minister of Education in the Province.

Now that's a bold move! Why did they do it? In part, they couldn't get the elected local school boards to get their heads into the issue of student learning and student performance, and get them out of the trivia of football fields, athletic schedules, and that kind of business. Many of the school boards were so hung up on those issues, they consumed all their time and energy with them, leaving nothing for the issues that really mattered—teaching and learning.

One colleague on a school board decided that he wasn't going to run for a second term. When I asked him why, he said his only agenda for getting on the board in the first place was to get soccer recognized as an interscholastic sport in his district. He had established that goal, so he was getting out. Do we need school board members with an attitude about their vested interests, and only that? We have to figure out a way to get them to be the leaders of the mission of the organization or we're going to be in trouble. If school boards are going to be around very long, they're going to have to become a proactive force for change.

You might say, "Well, maybe eliminating school boards can happen in Canada, but not in the United States."

Go to New Jersey! There are several districts in New Jersey where the locally elected board has been set aside. Instead, the state commissioner of education has appointed a superintendent who then reports directly to the state commissioner. There is no board of education. Again, either school boards need to become a positive, proactive, vision-driven force for change in their communities or they're likely to go out of business.

Another set of anchors would include administrators at all levels—superintendents, assistant superintendents, directors of programs, principals, assistant principals, and the like. They are the aristocracy of the system-in-place. When you are the aristocracy, near the top of the system, you've been the winner. When you try to sell organizational or system reform to the aristocrats of the system-in-place, it's a tough sell. It's like selling revolution to the ruling class!

The question administrators often ask me is, "If we were to restructure our schools and districts along the lines you're suggesting, can you guarantee me a position of equal or greater status than I enjoy right now?"

My answer is, "There are no guarantees."

Administrators then say, "Well, if you can't guarantee me equal status or better coming out the other side of restructuring of the system, why would I sign up for it?"

Needless to say, a lot of the resistance from change comes from the aristocrats who have benefited most from the system-in-place. They have to become a part of the change process, but it is true—we can't guarantee people the same kind of status as we begin to restructure the system.

The next major anchors are the unions, associations, and all other vested interest groups. In most states, the teachers' organization mirrors the pyramid model. The state-level organization matches the state department of education. The district level mirrors the school board. Building representatives are similar to principals. Rank-and-file members match up to the teaching staff at schools. The levels and silos apply here as well.

I'm not being anti-union by pointing this out. These groups came into being by organizing themselves around the system-in-place and matching it. Like the system-in-place, they will need to reinvent themselves, too.

Community should be viewed as plural—that is, communities. We have all kinds of communities—the parent community, the business community, the political community, the religious community, etc. Inside each community, you might have different racial/ethnic subgroups—African-American interest groups, Hispanic interest groups, Asian interest groups, and so forth. These are all part of the anchors to the system. If we're going to think about bringing change to the system, we have to make an exhaustive list of the anchors in the communities.

At your school and district level, identify the stakeholders. If you're going to err in any direction, err in the direction of being overly inclusive. I would rather have you recognize a subgroup as a legitimate stakeholder, and think about ways of bringing it into the change process, than run the risk of leaving it outside.

In many of the states where the reform effort has failed, it has been derailed by different vested interest groups. A Colorado district went through the ravages of having its reform effort derailed a few years ago when the board was recalled and a new board was put in. The superintendent was dismissed and the district backed out of all reforms. What went wrong? The people there underestimated the power of the system-in-place and underestimated the need to create a critical mass of support among the external stakeholders. Other jurisdictions are having the same problem. It behooves us to err in the direction of being overly inclusive, making sure all stakeholder groups are part of the change process.

If we're going to make change, we have to bring all of these anchors into the process. As Pat Dolan says, "In order to be able to move a system and change it, we have to create a new **we**."

We have to bring these people together in a collaborative process. The teachers' association, the administrators, the board, the community, and other stakeholder groups have to come together to see themselves as a new **we**. They can't come inside the room to represent their own interests only. Instead, they have to come in to collaborate and be willing to talk as equals.

The common denominator: we all have a stake in the future of this country and our children. We have to begin our discussion with that common ground. One of the first things the new **we** membership must do is seek permission and support for change.

Are there any nonnegotiables when it comes to change? I'd like to argue that, in this concept of a new **we**, in the best of all worlds, leave as much territory as possible for people to discover and design the new system. Don't constrain it. As soon as you start putting constraints on it, you limit the possibilities.

Chapter 7

The New We

Where do we begin the discussion with the new **we**? Dr. Russell Ackoff, a systems theorist at the Wharton School in Philadelphia, has introduced a concept called idealized redesign, which can be of tremendous value to us. Basically, idealized redesign is an unconstrained way for the people of the new **we** to come together to reinvent the system.

Imagine that we have gathered the new **we** around the interest in a single school. Imagine further that the very school we care so much about and have gathered to talk about has been completely destroyed overnight. You and your colleagues have been asked to redesign and rebuild that school without political, fiscal, regulatory, or legal constraint. What would you do differently?

When I ask teachers to engage in this process of redesign, I'm usually met with resistance for three reasons, each symptomatic of a problem in education.

Teachers say to me, "Look, Lezotte, why would you ask us to spend our time doing this idealized redesign? Our school was not destroyed last night!"

One of the problems with concrete sequential thinkers like this is their difficulty doing random abstract thinking. Developing an idealized and unconstrained vision for a school requires random abstract thought. Concrete sequential thinkers say, "Don't make me go to these planning meetings. Just tell me what to do and I'll do it. I want to be invited to the party, but I don't want to plan it. Just tell me what dish to bring."

I'll try to mollify this group by telling them they can't go to lunch until noon anyway, so just try to humor me and play the game. Usually, after a bit more resistance, they'll go along with it.

Teachers will also say to me, "Look, Lezotte, even if our school was completely destroyed last night, they wouldn't ask us to redesign and rebuild it."

This is symptomatic of how powerless the people at the bottom of the pyramid feel. I have to fight this by convincing them that, yes, they really want to know what you would do differently. The top of the pyramid really does want to hear from you.

A third group of teachers will say to me, "Even if our school was destroyed last night and, even if they did ask us to redesign and rebuild the system, it certainly wouldn't be without constraint."

Ackoff's answer to the teachers and planners who might take this position would be to ask them, "If you can't imagine what you would do differently in an unconstrained condition to make your system work better, what would make you think that you would be able to recognize an opportunity if it knocked on the door tomorrow?"

To paraphrase from an old Broadway musical, how are you ever going to have a dream come true, if you don't have a dream? If you don't have a vision of a better way, how are you going to be able to sort through opportunities that might come by?

What we need is to get people to dream the big dream in an unconstrained way at first. Then we can begin to say, "O.K., now how can we operationalize that?"

Ackoff gives us three criteria to pay attention to in order to be able to do an idealized redesign:

1 ▸ The redesign must be feasible.

Now you might say to me, "Wait a minute, Lezotte! You just told us the key to idealized redesign was to have it be unconstrained!"

Yes, I did. But here's what Ackoff means by feasible. The feasibility standard implies that it must be feasible with the knowledge we have at hand. It's not about money or rules or regulation. It's about knowledge.

2 ▸ The redesign must be sustainable.

There are millions and millions of dollars being spent each year on innovations in American public education, but not all innovations are sustainable.

One of the things school districts have become very good at is writing proposals to get grant money in order to do something they want to do. I ask administrators, "Why are you trying to get this grant from the state? What do you hope to accomplish with this grant?"

One of the things I'll most likely hear is, "If we get this grant, it will give us the resources to change the system-in-place!"

The problem is grants don't tend to change systems. Grants usually have a short lifetime—maybe two or three years. Grant money does drive new programs in a short-term way, but because it's short-term money, you keep that new program at the margin of the system. After all, you know when the money runs out, you're probably going to have to amputate the program. You don't want it to hemorrhage on the system.

I'm certainly not discouraging you from applying for and using grant money. What we need to think more about, though, is this issue of sustainability. That means we have to think in a long-term way. What if the program works? How are you going to be able to support it in year four, if you get a three-year grant? What are you going to do to keep it going?

That's the issue of sustainability.

3 ▶ **The redesign must be adaptable.**

The new system has to be able to learn from its own experience. It has to be a learning system.

One of the ways an organization makes a commitment to adaptability is in the way it trains and retrains its work force. If you want to atrophy in place, you don't spend time and effort training and retraining your work force.

Finance books in the world of the private sector recommend that, in order to maintain its viability in its market, an organization must be willing to spend seven to 10 percent of its resources on the renewal of its people, products, services, and system. This is just to stay even. It's a rare school district in America that spends as much as two percent of its resources on the renewal of its people, products, services, and system. No wonder it's so hard to get schools to change— they're investing so little in the change process!

Four qualities need to characterize an organization if it is going to make the kind of changes we need to see happen. At the base are human qualities. The human factors will dictate how well the new system is going to work and how effective it is going to be.

The first quality is **trust or trustworthiness**. There is no quality continuous improvement model without high levels of trust and trustworthiness.

The second quality is **empowerment**. You cannot empower a slave. You can only empower someone who is set free. People must feel free and sovereign before they're going to feel empowered.

Third, in this puzzle of human relationships, is a **sense of stewardship**. Public schools have evolved to answer the first set of questions: what are the implications for adults who work in schools? Now we need to answer the next set: what are the implications for children who learn in schools?

Finally, to go forward with a partnership based on collaboration, we have to set ground rules based on **civility**. Much of the organizational work going on right now is not being done in a very civil way. People are not being fair or honest with each other, and part of this is grounded in the issue of distrust.

Typically, in today's setting, a principal will go before the faculty and say, "Here's a plan for next year that our school teams are working on. We need to hear back from you right now about whether or not you have any concerns with this plan."

The faculty will look around, shift in their seats a bit, and give no feedback. The meeting will adjourn.

Case closed? Hardly. If you could make yourself invisible and follow the faculty out into the parking lot, you'd hear some interesting comments. "Did you hear what those fools want us to do next year? Are they crazy? How will that work or make any difference?"

What's it going to take to get the conversation out of the parking lot and into the meeting? It's going to take a strong sense of trust, empowerment, stewardship, and civility.

Chapter 8

The High-Tech/Communications/ Information School

One of the pieces of information that schools should collect when parents sign their children up for kindergarten is, "How many years of formal schooling does your child have prior to kindergarten?"

Now this may seem like a strange question to ask, but here's what we're starting to see across the country. Middle-class children in America tend to come to kindergarten with two years or more of formal school, usually in the form of nursery or preschool. Disadvantaged children in America tend to come to kindergarten with one year or less of formal school, usually in the form of daycare.

What argument can you possibly think of that says we ought to put these two different groups of children, with their different readiness for school, backgrounds, and prerequisites, into the same classroom—simply because they are all five years old? Age-based placement may have made sense under a mission of compulsory attendance with learning being optional, but if your mission is **Learning for All**, it just doesn't make sense any more.

Would a group of adults, who wanted to learn French, learn better if we placed them in classes according to their age, regardless of their prior experience in the French language? Should we place all adults who decide to take a computer course in groups according to their age, in spite of the fact that some of these students will have lots of experience with computers while others won't be quite sure where the "on" switch is?

Age-based placement is a leftover from our industrial society model. Alvin and Heidi Toffler, in their best-selling book, *The Third Wave*, give us a powerful framework of questions to ask to determine whether our system is a leftover from an earlier society. All organizations, including our schools, will need to ask these questions:

 Does your organization resemble a factory?

Is the innovation designed to make the factory model school or district run more efficiently? In other words, are you still treating everybody the same? Or, is your school designed to get rid of the factory model altogether and replace it with an individualized, customized educational system? Twenty-first century organizations will not look like factories.

 Does your organization continue to produce a mass society?

Factory model organizations mass-produced every product and service. They even created the masses. High-tech/communications/information institutions will require radically different kinds of workers. Educational institutions will be required to produce radically different kinds of learners with different knowledge and skills. The new society will favor individuality, as well as support entrepreneurial risk and teamwork. Workers will not be seen as easily interchangeable.

Education has to balance our approach. We want to assure that every child who comes through the system has a set of common core learnings. Literacy, for example, must be universal. At the same time, we want to have a system of education that allows us to diversify and play to the different talents and strengths each child possesses.

3   How many eggs are in the basket?

Remember, in our pyramid model, the authority in the system was at the top. A few people call all the shots. The rest of the folks down in the system are just the worker bees, following orders, and conducting their tasks.

Organizations in the future will have to decentralize to get more of the authority closer to the point of service delivery. Frontline workers will need to have more discretionary authority over the actions and decisions they have to make.

In schools, teachers working individually and in small groups will have to have much more authority in setting the process of education that we need to assure that all children can and do succeed. We'll need to spread the eggs out—the decision-making points can't just be concentrated at the top.

4   Is your organization vertical or virtual?

Factory model organizations accumulate more and more functions over time and get fat. They find it hard to suppress the impulse toward vertical integration. By contrast, high-tech/communications/information organizations subtract or subcontract functions and remain slim. They contract out as many of their tasks as possible.

School districts are going to have to reduce the tendency to take on more and more responsibility. The focus must be on the learning mission.

5 ▶ Does your organization empower the home?

The industrial revolution stripped most of the functions out of the home and away from the family. Work shifted from the home to the office or factory.

The new wave reempowers the family and the home. It restores many of the lost functions that once made the home so central to society. IBM in Chicago, for example, has been selling off office space because more and more of their workers are working out of their homes with computers, through the Internet and e-mail, and so on. Entertainment has moved to the home. Right now, you can get a movie on demand. Shopping has moved to the home. You can order just about anything from the comfort of your home.

Concepts like home schooling are becoming much more popular with computers and the Internet—and we haven't seen anything yet! It seems to me it would be smart to try to build an outreach capability with home school parents, so when they do decide to send their kids back to school, you have a chance of attracting them to your school. It does us very little good to see them as defectors or the enemy. Parents who are able to invest the kind of time and effort into assuring high levels of literacy for their children in the early years are going to be receptive to bringing their children into the school system later, for the use of laboratories, the advantage of cocurricular activities, and so on. They are potential partners to the new school system.

Chapter 9

Guiding Principles

With the vision of the new mission in our heads, I recommend focusing on these essential guiding principles for our schools as they move into the future:

Define the intention.

In the future, even more than in the past, schools and districts are going to have to be explicit about their intentions. During the old-style industrial society, we assumed everybody knew what knowledge, skills, and dispositions were associated with the educated person and success in the workplace. With the knowledge explosion at hand and easy access to modern technology, we cannot leave to chance what schools are to teach and students are to learn.

If school districts are going to survive, they will have to become more aggressive in specifying what it is they want the system to accomplish. One of the important changes is for the system to focus on learning and the learner, rather than on teaching and the teacher. What is it, more than anything else, that we want our kids to know, do, and be disposed to do as they move through their experiences in school?

Someone once made a comment to me that one of the characterizations of an effective school, as compared to other schools, is an intense, almost ruthless passion in the intention to teach all children the basic and essential school skills outlined as important. Intentionality is really the spine of the system.

The responsibility for meeting this standard must rest with the appropriate political body. For the time being, that means the local board of education. The board would be encouraged to consult with both internal and external experts, but in the end, it has to give intention, direction, and definition to the system.

Cherish diversity.

Factory model schools, in their assumption that learning could be mass-produced, looked at sameness and consistency as cherished norms. When such schools failed to achieve the expected levels of success for some students in some subjects, the blame was placed squarely at the feet of the uncooperative students who didn't fit the system.

Successful 21st century schools and districts will organize themselves around the standard of assumed diversity. They will recognize and be prepared to respond to the fact that learners will enter the system of schooling already different. They will proceed at different rates and will benefit from different types of teaching styles and settings. Individual differences in learners will no longer be seen as chance phenomena or even a nuisance; instead, such differences will be seen as the essence of what makes each individual unique.

For example, about half of the kids in a school may have access to a computer at home and half of them may not. The school has a limited number of computers and limited time available on them. How should the school best respond to that reality? One of the problems we're running into is that the first kids who get to use the computers the most at school are also the ones who have access to them at home. It seems almost un-American to try to limit computer usage for those have-it-at-home kids in favor of the ones who don't have access to the technology at home. But what are we to do? Adapting to the needs of the students is the only way to go.

In order to manage this high level of adaptability and flexibility, school districts of the future are going to have to be organized so that decisions are made closer to the point of actual service delivery. Concepts and strategies like site-based, shared decision making are not only desirable, but essential.

The district's role will center itself on the "what" questions. What is it we want our students to know, do, and be inclined to do when they graduate from our school district? The "how" questions will have to be left to the actual service providers. The board will have to accept responsibility for assuring that the staff has the knowledge, skills, and desire to deal with the diversity standard.

Expect and encourage individuality.

Mass production systems viewed the workers as being of equal worth and value, and interchangeable. To succeed in the new system, schools and districts are going to have to begin with the proposition that each worker is unique and special, and not easily exchanged with another person. The standard of individuality includes both the adults who work in the system and the students who are the customers of the system. After all, if the production function of the school is to produce learning, the students are the final workers in that process.

Creating schools and districts that honor the concept of individuality will require huge changes. For example, most collective bargaining agreements are based on the factory model. They tend to standardize everything from class size to compensation. As soon as we begin to acknowledge that each unit of labor is special, we'll have to go back to the drawing board to determine fair and just ways of acknowledging their individuality and unique contribution to the overall aims of the system.

Once we solve the problems of recognizing the importance of individuality as it relates to the paid employees of the system, we can then turn to the more difficult task of envisioning how individuality can work with the students. It is a must that every learner has an individualized education plan. Once we have met this standard, we need to carefully monitor and adjust it based on the success of the student— and we need to do this frequently enough to make a real difference in that student's learning.

Make use of technology.

In order to move toward the new mission, several technologies will have to be braided together to create this learning system. To use some of the language of W. Edwards Deming, the schools and districts of the future must develop systems based on the profound knowledge of the work they do. In our case, we are in the learning business. We need to base decisions on the profound knowledge of the human brain, human learning, and the cognitive sciences.

We'll need to know about child growth and development, and the social psychology of the group. In addition, schools and districts will need the latest information-processing technology to maintain the system. Finally, boards are going to have to invest heavily in continuing lifelong learning of the workers. Likewise, workers are going to have to accept more personal responsibility for their own professional growth and development.

Chapter 10

Customization is Key

The key to survival of the 21st century school district will be its ability and willingness to customize service on a continuous and immediate basis. We have come to expect customized service in virtually every other sector of our life. We shouldn't settle for anything less when it comes to the education of our children or grandchildren!

So how do we create a system that has the capability of managing such a task? Perhaps the easiest way for us to begin to create such a system is to strip it back to its most basic unit—the single learner. Assume that you have all of the resources available to you that you currently have, but you only have one child to teach. How would you design the system?

If you think about this for a few minutes, some answers quickly come to mind:

1 I'm sure that you would first determine where the child fits on the curricular maps that you have been asked to teach. You would begin by assessing the prerequisites (which implies that you know what they are).

2 You would bring the curriculum to the learner. You would want to know how to make meaningful connections to that learner, so that he or she will find purpose in the new information.

3 You would fit the pace of instruction to the learner's pace, moving him or her along fast enough to avoid boredom, but slow enough to assure learning. You would want to frequently monitor and adjust, to be as sure as possible that you are on the right course.

These steps, taken together, constitute a system designed to manage massive customization of service.

I suppose you're concerned about the fact that there is more than one student in your classes. The best way to proceed to deal with the larger number is to begin by simply adding one student, so there are now two. What changes would you have to make in the processes just described to accommodate the 100 percent increase in class size? Having two students means that you have to contend with individual differences, but it can also mean that one student can sometimes be an additional resource for the other.

My experience in working with teachers by starting the process with one student, then adding a second, a third, and so on, has been that when we get to learning groups of more than six, the old factory model kicks in and blocks the mind-set of the teacher. Up to that point, the teacher can imagine that, with tools like computers and other technologies, service can be customized. Because of this "mind block," the organizing structure of the school of the future cannot be the classroom of 25 to 30 students. Instead, it must be the six-person, flexible learning microcommunity.

Are there any examples of systems that can manage customization of service at a level like that facing the typical school? There sure are, all around us! My favorite example is the air travel industry, probably because my work requires me to fly frequently.

Imagine this scenario: I'm going to Austin, Texas from Detroit, Michigan. First of all, my travel agent is quick to tell me that I have several options, some of which are more convenient for me than others. I make my selection and the ticket is cut. I present that ticket at the counter and I'm assigned a seat, a gate, a time of departure, and, if I'm lucky, my luggage will go with me.

I'll be on a plane with over 150 people, each of whom will have an individualized flight plan. Some of those on the plane will have started their journey in a place other than Detroit, and some will go on to other flights after they arrive in Austin.

What happens if the schedule doesn't work out and I miss a connection somewhere? Usually adjustments are made, a new plan is set, and I'm on my way again.

Here's another example. Recently, my wife and I decided to enter into a lease for a car. We had never leased a car before and were quite surprised at the many different options available in the leasing process. You can, in a sense, have a customized lease based on how many miles you feel you need to drive, how long you want to keep the car, what kind of features you want it to have, etc.

What's the difference between the air travel and car leasing examples of customization and the situation facing a school, where you have to pick up the learners where they are in the system and move them on to the next levels of learning? Like the airlines and the auto industry, schools won't be able to manage such massive customization of service without the aid of computers and other supportive technology. Schools also won't be able to manage such customization until we abandon the factory model and turn to the new mission.

There was a study done recently out of Harvard on charter schools. The question the researchers asked was, "When people choose to send their children to a charter school, what do they truly believe they are going to get from the charter school that they're not currently getting from a public school?"

There are a few people who want to use charter schools as a way of resegregating, so their kids don't have to go to school with children who are different because of issues such as race, ethnicity, or poverty. That case is not going to win the day. The United States is not going to surrender its commitment to equity and fairness by allowing people to use charter schools as a way of resegregating.

The majority of people sending their children to charter schools, though, truly believe they are getting something beyond what their public schools can give. First, they believe the charter school will be more responsive to them as customers. Second, they believe the charter school will be more willing to customize service to meet the needs of individual children.

Is there any reason public schools cannot make this same commitment? If we are going to begin to see parents and their children as customers, we're going to have to be willing to revisit all of our policies, programs, and practices. We need to begin to establish a climate of diversification of services to really meet the needs of individuals.

Without prior notice, a parent of a child in the system ought to be able to call the superintendent and ask him or her how well that child is doing relative to the mastery of the intended curriculum of the school district. The superintendent should be able to turn to a computer at the side of his or her desk, call up the performance record of that child, and describe in detail how well the child is doing in mastering the curriculum.

The technology exists to meet this standard; the issue is the commitment to do so.

Why is it important for the superintendent to be able to make the connection to an individual student on demand? First of all, if the superintendent can make the connection between his or her office and a single student, anyone between the superintendent and the student can do the same. The principal could be called and asked the question, or the teacher or guidance counselor of the student could be called. This gives the system the vertical reach that is needed. Everyone who has control of resource allocations must be able to connect with the learning mission in this way.

Second, if the superintendent can be asked about any single child on demand, the superintendent can also be asked about groups of children (girls as a group compared to boys as a group, etc.). This gives the system the necessary horizontal reach.

The vertical and horizontal connections provide the basic elements needed to effectively manage the learning mission of the school district. Most districts have the technical capability to manage the money and attendance mission in this manner. In fact, a school superintendent I know spoke for 99 percent of the school districts in America today when he told me, "We have a system in our district to manage our money down to the dime, but we don't have a system for managing the learning mission."

The effective school district of the future is going to have to extend that capability to the new mission of compulsory learning. The proper use of technology will be critical if the quality district is going to be able to engage in the self-monitoring and adjustment processes that are a part of a dynamic and responsive organization.

Chapter 11

The Effective School Improvement Process

I well remember the early days of effective schools research. As a member of the original team of researchers—including the renowned Dr. Wilbur Brookover at Michigan State University and well-known pioneer in the effective schools movement, the late Ron Edmonds—I can honestly state that, when we found effective schools out there (in nature, as it were), they were already effective. We didn't have a clue as to how they had gotten that way. When educators came to us for advice on how to make their schools effective, too, we knew we needed to develop a set of procedures.

We sat down together and started looking at these schools, examining the processes they were using, and determining the common ground. We also looked at successful models in other arenas. This may surprise you, but the two most effective change models we identified to give us guidance on setting the improvement process were Weight Watchers and Alcoholics Anonymous. If you look at the data, these two groups share many qualities in common. They provide members with steps and stages for sustainable change.

As a result of our studies and over 25 years of experience, we were able to come up with steps and stages that work to help make schools more effective. I'm confident that, if schools choose to use this framework and thoughtfully work through the process, they can be assured of good success.

Our school improvement process, outlined in detail in my workbook, *A Guide to the School Improvement Process based on Effective Schools Research*, consists of five stages:

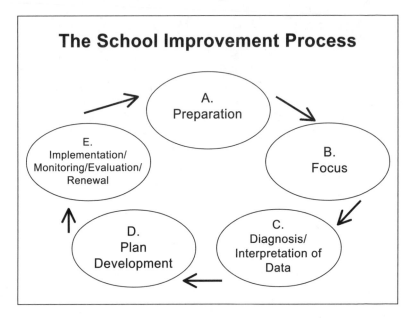

Many schools are already engaged in a planning process and the last thing I would suggest is to abandon good work already happening. Instead, I'm hoping you'll look at the model we have to offer and place yours against it. If necessary, you may want to augment what you are currently doing to include that step or those stages that may be missing from your process.

A natural question for you to ask is, "Why should we use the effective schools framework?"

I can give you five good reasons:

This model for school change and development is based on and supported by the research—research that has been accumulating and strengthening the case since the 1960's.

This model focuses specifically on student achievement. It's about student learning and student performance.

The effective schools process pays simultaneous attention to issues of quality and equity. I think it's fair to say that, we, as a nation, are committed to both. Our founding fathers and mothers didn't say, "Quality or equity—take your pick." Rather, they said that, as a nation, we are committed simultaneously to the policy pillars of quality and equity, and our public school system rests on those twin pillars. An improving school can demonstrate the increasing presence of equity in quality.

The model is collaborative in form, recognizing that improving a school requires cooperation among administrators, teachers, support staff, and parents. It cannot be done just by administrative decree. People have to believe in the mission and core values, and be willing to sign up to take the action steps that will lead to success.

The model is ongoing and self-renewing.

The good news is you can start anytime you want!

The bad news is you will never finish.

But this makes all the sense in the world! The journey to school improvement is just that—an ongoing, self-renewing journey. As human beings, we will likely never reach the destination known as perfection. We certainly can, though, keep moving along the path to continuous improvement.

Chapter 12

Getting Ready

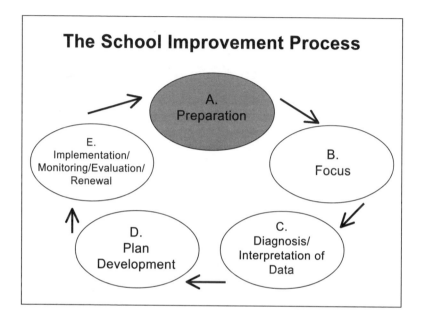

What do we need to do to get ready for school improvement?

The first step is to identify a laundry list of stakeholder groups. We've identified the anchors in the system—the school board, the administrators, the teachers, the vested interest groups. We're also aware that external stakeholders must be included in the discussion, including parents, businesspeople, community leaders, political leaders, religious leaders, senior citizens, and all others who have an interest in the school's impact on the community.

Remember this: whoever is not brought in on what you're doing in the beginning will likely be down on what you're doing later! They will pick the time and place to bushwhack your efforts. In a number of places around the country where school reform has been derailed, the opposition has usually come in the form of a small, well-organized external stakeholder group. In general, if paid educators have to go head-to-head in argument against school reform with a well-organized group from the right or left, the paid educators are going to lose almost every time. If you want to insure against failure downstream, then the very first part of your preparation stage must be to identify the stakeholders and bring them into the process.

Two researchers from Stanford University, David Tyack, a historian, and Larry Cuban, a policy analyst, have written a book, *Tinkering Toward Utopia*, that gives us an insight into the challenges ahead as we try to involve stakeholders in the improvement process. Numerous initiatives to try to reform the schools have been advocated by people they call the "policy talkers." The policy talkers might be elected officials or scholars who advocate different positions. The policy talkers can talk all they want, and advance the most innovative reforms, but most Americans have developed a mental model that is very difficult to overcome.

This model of the "real school" has become deeply entrenched in our society. It's based on what Tyack and Cuban call the "rules of grammar" for what a real school is like:

In the minds of the American people, a real school is a school that starts in September and goes until June.

A real school is a school that starts at 8:00 in the morning and runs until 3:00 or so in the afternoon.

A real school is open Monday through Friday.

A real school places kids in learning groups based on age.

A real school talks about grade levels.

Does all of this look very familiar?

Parents and teachers will allow you to do different things with students around their learning goals, as long as you don't change the rules of grammar of the real school. For example, if you want to do an after-school program for a cross-age group of children, there would be very little resistance. It's after school, so it's outside the rules of a real school. If you start trying to do that same thing during the school day, though, you're now messing with the rules of grammar of a real school, and parents and teachers will become very concerned.

We have a definite problem confronting those deeply held rules of grammar that so characterize our experiences in schools, including the ones we ourselves attended. When you start changing systems, processes, and cultures—as you must do to create a school for compulsory **Learning for All**—you come up against the grammar of the real school. How do you confront these rules? Once you know who your stakeholders are, you need to develop a strategy for orienting them to the effective schools process.

That means people have to learn and understand the language of effective schools. What does the research say? What does it mean to be committed to a process of continuous school improvement based on that research?

Identify how you're going to make contact with your stakeholder groups and how you're going to invite them to become part of the discussion. The methods you use to do this may differ from community to community, but there are tools to help you in the form of books, software, and videos. At the very least, I suggest the following:

- Conduct a needs assessment to become more aware of the attitudes your various stakeholder groups hold toward the school and to identify specific problem areas.

- Introduce the effective schools correlates.

- Review student outcome test data to provide the rationale and needed impetus for undertaking the school improvement effort.

- Give an outline of the big picture, briefly describing the steps and stages of the effective schools process.

- Make it clear that time will be required to develop and carry out the resulting improvement plan. There are no quick fixes; improvement may take two or three years to become apparent.

- Stress that the goal for teachers is to become more effective in their jobs and, consequently, more satisfied with their work.

Be aware that there will be a need for discussion time after the initial overview—and the larger the school, the more time the discussion will take up. Expect this readiness phase to take a month or even several. It's critical not to rush it.

After identifying and involving stakeholders, and orienting them to the process, the next step is to create a leadership group. You may want to call it the school improvement team, the school effectiveness team, the school reform team, or whatever works best in your situation. Obviously, every single stakeholder can't be actively involved in all parts of the process—it would be too bulky and cumbersome, and very little would get done. Therefore, your team must be able to stand the test of "representativeness." People from any stakeholder group should be able to look at the composition of the team and feel that it is representative of them. That means parents must be on the team, administrators must be on the team, teachers must be on the team, support staff must be on the team, and so on.

The expectation is that, over time, all internal stakeholders (teachers, administrators, support staff) will have the opportunity to participate in the team process. This creates something of a dilemma for the principal. Just because the faculty elects a representative doesn't mean the representative will reflect the interests of all faculty members. Maybe the younger teachers will feel disenfranchised; maybe the senior teachers will feel left out. Maybe the elected representative will reflect the majority, but not the minority. Though the election process is a democratic one, at another level, it doesn't assure the kind of representation we really want.

The principal may say, "Rather than risk an electoral process that creates a biased group, what I think I'll do is select the school improvement team myself. That way, I can make sure we have the mix of gender, race/ethnicity, and internal and external stakeholders that I want."

The problem here is you'll never be able to rise above the argument that the team consists of handpicked favorites of the principal. You're caught between a rock and a hard place, so what do you do?

The answer, I think, is to initiate discussions to come up with a slate of people across grade levels, seniority levels, gender, race/ethnicity groups, etc. Negotiate here and there to substitute one person for another, if necessary, before you take the slate out for endorsement by the whole faculty. But then give the faculty the opportunity to certify and endorse that slate as representative of their interests. The most important thing in the long run is to have a broad cross section.

One of the things I've seen happen during the development of school teams is the most enthusiastic and energized people are selected, while people who are negative or indifferent are left out. Certainly, it's a temptation to go with enthusiastic people only and tell them to provide leadership. The challenge comes, though, when the team must turn over the key of ownership to the rest of the people. The "early adopters" lack patience to wait for the "slow adopters" to come along.

There are three kinds of people in your school right now. One group is those early adopters I just mentioned. They're eager for change, ready for new ideas, enthusiastic, and all set to go. You can easily get this group on the bus.

The second group consists of laggards. They're not "negative." They just need more time, more information, more understanding, and more discussion.

The third group is the out-and-out resisters. These people are content with where they are and they're simply not going to budge.

The key to success with a change effort is to concentrate on the second group, the laggards. When the laggards have enough time, information, understanding, and opportunity for discussion, they will begin to lean forward. Once that happens, the principal, leader, or chairperson of the school improvement team should announce that the bus is leaving the station and all aboard who're getting aboard!

After creating a team, it's critical to supply training. As a rule, schools are not very collaborative in nature. It would be a mistake to assume team members even know the dynamics for group decision making and problem solving. Sure signs that training is needed include apathy, conflicts, confusion, low participation, and high dependency on or negative reactions to the team leader.

While there is no one way to do team training, suggestions include targeted sessions conducted by your district's staff development coordinator or the appropriate person from your county's educational service agency. Collaborative workshops with other districts with similar needs may also work. The objectives are to develop a group mission statement; establish team member roles and responsibilities; outline conflict management procedures; examine the team's problem-solving strategies; and improve communication and listening skills.

I would also suggest setting up guidelines to structure and organize team meetings. Establish a regular schedule for meetings and stick to it. Provide realistic agendas with specific goals for each meeting, and give stakeholders plenty of opportunity to have input into those agendas. Keep minutes, make sure each member has a copy, and post them in a highly visible area for all interested parties to read.

The principal has a particularly important role to play on the team and that is to be there! The team needs you. Clear the deck to make sure team meetings are a priority. Be ready to take an objective look at practices in your school.

Chapter 13

The Right Focus

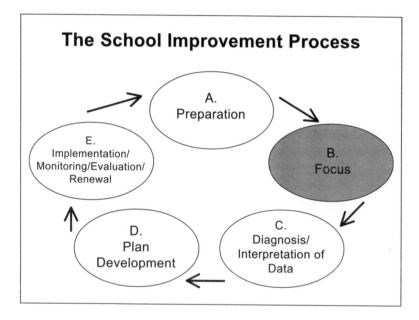

The School Improvement Process

A. Preparation

B. Focus

C. Diagnosis/Interpretation of Data

D. Plan Development

E. Implementation/Monitoring/Evaluation/Renewal

I'm willing to bet most schools today have a mission statement. However, I'm also willing to bet that very few schools have a sense of mission—an energized commitment from all people involved in the process. The new mission of **Learning for All** requires that kind of commitment.

A clear mission statement provides a focus to your efforts and can be thought of as the foundation of your plan. First, your school district, as a strategic organization, must set the mission for the district. Then, your school, as an operational unit responsible for delivering the goals of the strategic organization, must develop its particular sense of mission inside the district's overall mission.

Many books have been written on developing mission statements, so I won't try to tell you how you need to do it, beyond giving this advice. Every mission statement should provide answers to these questions:

 1 Who will deliver the service?

2 Who will benefit?

3 What is the nature of the service?

4 What constitutes observable evidence of mastery?

5 What is the level of accountability?

At this Focus stage of school improvement, you must begin with the end in mind. What is it that we want kids to know, do, and be disposed to do when they finish 12th grade?

Break it down further. What is it that we want kids to know, do, and be disposed to do when they finish 5th grade?

Take the question to your stakeholders. What does our public want students to know, do, and be disposed to do when they finish their time with us?

The development of a clear statement of the essential student learnings of a school is probably one of the most difficult tasks in the Focus process, but it is essential. Without it, how will teachers know how to allocate instructional time, conduct appropriate task analyses, or give proper emphasis to reteaching? This step alone, if done well, will do much to assure future student success!

After a school clarifies its essential student learnings, I believe it is critical to the effective schools movement to identify subpopulations. You are effective for whom?

There are three subpopulations in schools today. The first is based on gender. We need to look at boys as a group compared to girls as a group.

The second has to do with race and ethnicity. Do the minority students, as a group, have access to participate in and benefit from our programs of curriculum and instruction in proportion to nonminority students?

The third subpopulation is based on socioeconomic status, which includes home and family background. Do the children who come to our schools from economically disadvantaged backgrounds, as a group, participate in and benefit from our programs of curriculum and instruction in proportion to our nondisadvantaged kids?

These three variables—gender, race/ethnicity, and socioeconomic status—represent the major gaps in student achievement in our country. If I had to weigh in on one, I would say that socioeconomic status represents the single biggest explanation of gaps in achievement. A major challenge will be to show more success for more of the economically disadvantaged students.

We must stop looking at schools in terms of the processes they utilize and start looking at them in terms of the results they are getting. For the last 100 years, we've judged schools as being good or bad based on inputs and processes. Regional accreditation programs have asked schools to extensively document their processes—how many books are in the school library, what is the amount of square feet in the science lab, etc.? They never confronted the question of whether the children were learning what it is we want them to be able to know and do!

The shift in mission has precipitated a shift in orientation toward judging schools. The first step in trying to do an analysis of whether a school is effective is to look at evidence of student learning and student performance.

How do we look at the achievement data? Do we just look at it in the average? The problem with that is you lose so much information! It's practically devoid of meaning.

If you have half of the children in the school scoring near 100 on an exam and the other half scoring near 50, averaging it out gives the school a score of 75. If you report out to the public that your school averages 75 on the test, even though you know full well that half of the kids failed it and the other half did very well, are you not misleading people? You need to look at that data in ways to get the most meaning out of it.

What ought to be the measure of school improvement? Student results—performance outcomes! The school must know what it is that it wants the kids to know and be able to do. The school must be intentional in setting out to teach kids the required curricula and in making sure they learn it. That's what I mean by outcomes or results or evidence of learning! We must have evidence that we gather from time to time to determine whether the kids have learned what we set out to have them learn.

Let's imagine that you hired me as your consultant to help you make a judgment about whether your school is effective. How would I proceed?

First, I would ask you, as faculty and local owners of a given school, "What will you accept as evidence of quality?"

You might say back to me, "We believe that we're a quality school because we have a high percentage of our students participating in advanced placement courses of study."

I would then ask, "Who participates in those quality programs?"

If I go inside your advanced placement math course, for example, and see that 78 percent of the students in that course are boys and the rest are girls, I would conclude that you may have good evidence of quality overall, but when you take the data apart on gender, you do not have proportional rates of participation by boys and girls.

One of the goals for your school, then, might be to ask, "What can we do to get more girls as a group to participate in advanced placement math courses?"

That would be a commitment to well-targeted, doable school reform.

What this Focus stage requires from you, then, is a clear mission statement, the identification of what you consider essential student learnings, and a careful analysis of your subpopulations. You are effective at what? You are effective for whom?

Chapter 14

Disaggregate and Diagnose

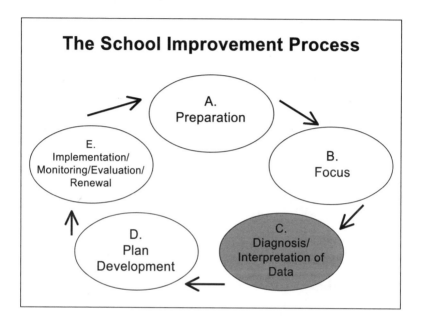

The School Improvement Process

- A. Preparation
- B. Focus
- C. Diagnosis/ Interpretation of Data
- D. Plan Development
- E. Implementation/ Monitoring/Evaluation/ Renewal

If you were working on a long-term basis with me as a consultant, you'd probably feel like running me out of town. You would say, "I am so sick and tired of hearing Lezotte ask us over and over again to 'show me the data, show me the data!'"

The reason I harp on this is I've learned in my work with school improvement that teachers and administrators often carry mental models of a reality that doesn't exist. The worst thing that could happen by looking at the data is that it confirms your mental model and you went through a little extra effort to prove it. The best thing that could happen by looking at the data is that you get a more accurate picture of the problem. More often than not, what I find is people look at the data and say, "Oh, my goodness, I never believed this was true! I didn't realize this was happening!"

Schools need to study the data to provide a benchmark for judging the impact of improvement efforts. First, student achievement data must be studied closely over time. Second, you have to look at the organizational dimensions of the school itself, to step back and see if the school contains the features necessary for effectiveness.

We also need to break the data down, so we can look at girls as a group, boys as a group, minority students as a group, and so on. Interestingly enough, I've heard educators say their school achievement level is low, but at least it's equal among groups. Boy and girls perform at comparable levels and, for some reason, they're content with that type of equity. Well, that's not going to cut it! The first standard that must be in place is high levels of achievement overall. The second standard is no differences in the distribution of that achievement across the major subsets of the student population.

Twenty-five years ago, this talk about disaggregating student data was rarely heard. Most schools, if they reported out anything by way of performance or results on any of their scores, looked at median measures or measures of central tendency. They could say, "We're doing a good job because our kids are scoring at the 50th percentile." But that score can be very misleading! Which kids scored above that? Which kids scored below it?

Most of our nation's schools have slowly come to the realization that disaggregating student data on the basis of gender is worth doing. Now, when we see school reports, it's common to see how girls are doing as a group compared to boys.

With even more reluctance, schools are beginning to disaggregate the data on the basis of race/ ethnicity. We're beginning to see, in the reports and test data, how minority students as a group look in comparison to nonminority students.

As a guideline, I would suggest that any group that comprises at least 20 percent of your student population should be disaggregated. If you find that one of the groups falls significantly below the others in student outcomes, please be assured that it doesn't mean your school is doing something purposefully bad for that group. It simply means your school is not succeeding for that group now. You have to identify the problem before you can identify the solution, and that's what makes disaggregation such a powerful tool!

Unfortunately, the greatest reluctance in the United States today is to disaggregate the student performance and achievement data based on socioeconomic status. I think the reason behind this is, at a deep level, school people don't believe poor kids can learn. That's one of the major mind-sets I'm trying to challenge through this whole process of school development. All children can learn—if we're willing to set the conditions in the school to assure that they do.

I would not recommend that a school disaggregate on the basis of race/ethnicity unless the school is willing to go on and also disaggregate data on the basis of socioeconomic status. If you are unwilling to do this, you are playing to racism on all sides of the racial line.

If you disaggregate data on the basis of race/ ethnicity, and you put out a graph that shows how the white children are doing and how the African-

American children are doing, in most cases, it's going to look like the white children are doing considerably better.

If you don't go on to disaggregate on the basis of socioeconomic status, the white people are going to say, "See, I told you so."

If you don't go on to disaggregate on the basis of socioeconomic status, the black people are also going to say, "See, I told you so."

However, their theory of cause is completely different!

Whites will see the gap and say, "I thought that the African-American people couldn't learn. See, that's what this shows."

African-Americans will look at the gap and say, "See, I told you that the system, the school, discriminated."

Here are the facts as I've come to know them. If you disaggregate on the basis of race/ethnicity and then again on the basis of socioeconomic status, I'll bet you'll find that middle-class white children's achievement looks more like middle-class black children's achievement than middle-class black children's achievement looks in comparison to poor black children's achievement.

Disaggregate the data at your school and call me if you disagree. I'm saying the biggest explanation of the gaps in student achievement today is grounded in socioeconomic status. It's not grounded, in the first instance, in race/ethnicity.

The biggest single indicator we have found over the years for indexing socioeconomic status of children in school is the highest education level of the parents, with preference given to indexing socioeconomic status to the education level of the mother. Schools that do a disaggregation on socioeconomic status usually use no more than a three-way division on education level. The mother without a high school diploma would be in the lowest socioeconomic group. The mother with a diploma would be in the middle socioeconomic group. The highest category would be the mother with some college or beyond.

By the way, in urban and rural schools, the single most frequent category of the three is going to be high school graduate. The next highest category is going to be less than a high school graduation, and the smallest category will be some college and beyond. If you go to the suburbs and do the same kind of an analysis, the largest category is still going to be high school grad, but the next largest is going to be college and beyond. The smallest category is going to be less than a high school diploma.

When you disaggregate your data, you can begin to learn a lot about what's working (or not working). Some of you may say to me, "Well, we disaggregated our data and it didn't tell us what to do."

Disaggregating data is not a problem-solving strategy. Rather, it's a problem-finding strategy. I certainly don't apologize for that! All of the problem-solving models I have studied start with a definition of the problem. Disaggregating student performance and learning data is the best way to attempt to describe and identify the nature of the problem.

Are you restricted in any way to disaggregating only to gender, race/ethnicity, and socioeconomic status? Of course not! Disaggregating data, as a process, is appropriate for allowing you to test any theory of cause.

If, for example, you have teachers in your school who believe that the reason some kids do not do well in school is because they come from single-parent homes, you can test that hypothesis. Disaggregate your student achievement data to show students coming from single-parent homes versus students coming from two-parent homes. Disaggregation of data allows you to look at any variable that people in the school or district believe is driving or influencing student achievement.

I worked with an urban district in the South that disaggregated the data by these two variables. They found that the highest-achieving group in the district was white females from middle-class, single-parent homes. It shows that you can't just cling to an old hypothesis. Single-parentness in middle-class homes had very little influence. However, if you add poverty to single-parentness, it's like one plus one equals three. You get a combining effect that does diminish achievement.

Let's say another competing hypothesis about gaps in achievement comes from the fact that some people believe it has to do with attendance. Those kids who come to school regularly everyday, on time, and who participate in a full sense in the curriculum and instructional program will do better on the measurements. Those kids who miss large amounts of school won't do quite as well. Now, if that's true, one of the ways we can show it would be to use attendance rates as the variable on which we disaggregate. We could look at students who missed

10 days or less of school last year versus students who missed 11 days or more. Study the achievement rates by those categories and you'll get a sense of the extent to which attendance is a factor influencing student achievement.

Disaggregation is a very powerful tool that can help you find and frame the problems in a school. What it does, more than anything else, is force people to stop looking simply at processes and start looking at results or outcomes.

Each school has to look at itself in context. Take the time to look at the data and get indicators. When you start to pull this together, remember the goal. We're trying to answer the question of who's profiting, and by how much, through our current programs of curriculum and instruction. Once we answer that question, we can identify our problem areas and develop our plans for improvement.

Chapter 15

Leading Indicators

I've asked you to spend a good deal of time disaggregating data as part of the Diagnosis stage of school improvement, but I'm going to risk telling you that my quality guru, W. Edwards Deming, believes it's almost impossible to improve a system by simply studying the results you're getting and trying to effect change based on your analysis of results. Frustrated? Upset? Confused? Are you thinking, "Why is Lezotte taking us on this wild ride anyhow?"

First, Deming is right. But hang in there, because I'm also right! You have to understand where you are going in terms of goals and objectives. You have to understand where you are on that journey to those goals and objectives, given your philosophy and mission. Disaggregation is still part of the analysis. For a system like a school to improve, however, you must not only monitor it by studying the data, you must also go back to the profound knowledge to understand where to go next. This is what Deming is telling us!

The correlates or characteristics of effective schools are one aspect of the profound knowledge that schools can use to help better themselves in terms of student learning and student performance.

Let me borrow a couple of concepts from the economist to help shed light on the profound knowledge base. The economist speaks of trailing and leading indicators. Picture a child pulling a little red wagon. The wagon may be thought of as the trailing inidicator and the child as the leading indicator. If you want to change where the little red wagon ends up, what do you do? Obviously, you need to negotiate with the child. Likewise, if you want to alter the learning outcomes for students in your school, you have to identify and modify the "drivers" or leading indicators of those outcomes.

Student learning, as evidenced by student performance, is a trailing indicator. As Deming said, studying trailing indicators won't allow you to improve the system. Schools are going to have to know what leading indicators drive the trailing indicators. School leaders are going to have to manage the leading indicators if schools are going to achieve their mission.

Let me give a simple example. Student performance on a reading test may be used by your district as an indicator of literacy. If schools are going to move toward the **Learning for All** mission, they can't simply watch the test scores and make changes after the fact. They need to watch the scores, anticipate the needs, and intervene before the tests are given.

What school leaders are going to have to know and respond to are the leading indicators that drive the test scores. For example, other things being equal, increasing time on task will drive changes in the trailing indicator of reading performance. Therefore, the school needs to be paying close attention to the variable of time and its uses.

School districts are going to have to develop a system for bringing the knowledge base of education to the school and all its faculty. That means having someone in the central office who is responsible for finding the profound knowledge and making it easily available to the school in a form that is useful to the teacher. Internet and intranet systems provide immediate access to the latest research and descriptions of proven practices.

Some may argue that school-level people will not take advantage of this information system because they haven't in the past. I wouldn't worry about this. As soon as learning is no longer optional and continuing contracts for all employees turn on the schools' and teachers' abilities to show results, the knowledge base to improve practice will become very popular! The tools are out there. My office has been publishing a compilation of the knowledge base for over a decade called the *Effective Schools Research Abstracts* and a computerized version called the *Effective Schools Research Assistant*™. The knowledge is out there—it's just a matter of making it common knowledge and, as a result, common practice!

The Diagnosis stage of school improvement requires educators to look carefully at the organizational dimensions of their school. The good news is the first generation correlates, the original seven correlates of effective schools, remain valid. If you are new to the discourse on effective schools and just beginning the journey, you'll want to pay close attention to the first generation correlates. Each school has to find where it is on this journey and move from there.

The original correlates also remain essential. We don't believe you can effectively get to the second generation correlates unless you are able to substantiate and manage the first generation correlates in your school. It's like building a two-story home. The original correlates are the first floor of that home. You have to build that infrastructure first in order to support the second story or the second generation.

Successful implementation of both the first and second generation correlates is an example of using the leading indicator model to try to drive effective change in the schools. Both of these, taken together, will move you toward the **Learning for All** mission.

This shows Ron Edmonds' original five correlates on one side and the Connecticut Department of Education's seven correlates on the other side:

Edmonds' Five Correlates	Connecticut Department of Education's Seven Correlates
• Safe and Orderly Environment	• Safe and Orderly Environment
• Instructional Leadership	• Instructional Leadership
• Climate of High Expectations for Success	• Climate of High Expectations for Success
• Frequent Monitoring of Student Progress	• Frequent Monitoring of Student Progress
• Pupil Acquisition of Basic Skills	• Clear and Focused Mission • Opportunity to Learn and Student Time on Task • Home-School Relations

There is a one-to-one correspondence between the first four correlates of Edmonds' original model and our working model of seven. A safe and orderly environment, instructional leadership, climate of high expectations for success, and frequent monitoring of student progress are just as essential then as now.

So how did we get from Edmonds' five to seven? One of the things you'll notice is that Edmonds' fifth factor was called "pupil acquisition of basic skills." Schools that were effective had a dominant focus on this, but what we found through subsequent research was it manifested itself in separate dimensions. One of the ways in which a school manifests its focus is on stating it through its clear and focused mission. The original schools Edmonds studied had that focus, and were able to mouth the mission. What we found, though, is that it's one thing for a school to be able to state that mission in a clear and focused way and quite another to live it! This may surprise you, but some people say one thing and do another! We found it necessary to say that the focus on basic school skills really needs to be thought about as a two-tiered variable:

 What does the school say that it cares most about? What is its shared sense of mission and purpose?

Does it walk its talk? Do the opportunities to learn, grouping practices, time allocations, and so forth reinforce the mission?

Now, when we go into a school, instead of asking generally about the focus, we ask about the shared, stated sense of mission and how it is verbalized. We also collect data on whether or not that state of purpose is manifested in the way classrooms operate day to day and week to week.

The unique seventh correlate that had no comparable connection in the original five-factor model is home/school relations. In the effective school, there is a strong partnership with the home.

You now can understand the evolution of how the dialogue on the correlates moved from the original five-factor model to the seven-factor model.

Chapter 16

The Correlate Continuum

What are some of the lessons we've learned over the years with respect to each correlate?

Safe and Orderly Environment

The concept of a safe and orderly environment still means the school atmosphere is orderly, purposeful, business-like, and free from the threat of physical harm. The school climate is not oppressive, and is conducive to teaching and learning. We've learned that changing the level of safety and orderliness in a school is one of the easier correlates to effect, if you can get a couple of prerequisites in place.

First, you must get all of the adults, but most particularly the teachers, to subscribe to the proposition that they are on duty, all the time, everywhere, while at work. Do a mental walk through a day in the life of your school or through the physical plan of your school. The first time you come to a place in the day or a place in the building where students might legitimately perceive that a teacher is not on duty, that's my nomination for a trouble spot.

What are some examples in real-world terms of how this could play itself out? In some schools, teachers are responsible for the discipline in their classroom. Somebody else, usually an administrator, is responsible for the discipline everywhere else. If that understanding starts to operate in your school, what we can predict is you're going to have a disciplinary climate problem into perpetuity! We have to get our teachers to subscribe to the proposition that they're on duty all the time—from the moment their cars arrive in the parking lot until they leave at the end of day. If they see misconduct in the hall, on the playground, or wherever, they are going to respond to it.

Data gathered through the Public Agenda surveys out of New York in the last few years indicate the number one concern expressed by parents is always around the issue of safety and orderliness. Are their children safe? You're not going to be able to go on and do much about the learning environment of a school unless you can establish and maintain a safe and orderly environment.

The second prerequisite is to get all the adults to subscribe to the proposition that they will behave with consistency around the agreed-upon rules and regulations of the school. If you have liberal teachers on the east end of your building who define tardiness by one standard and conservative teachers on the west end who define tardiness by another standard, what can we predict for your school? Not only will you have a tardiness problem into perpetuity, it will probably escalate into a distributed justice problem, with students crying, "This place isn't fair!"

How many rules should a school have? If you go to the research, you'll see that it's better for a school to have a few rules, consistently and evenhandedly enforced, then to have many rules unevenly implemented and haphazardly applied.

Sometimes educators quickly say, "Of course, that's true, because the kids would not be able to keep a lot of rules straight in their heads."

Here's my point: the students in a school could learn 72 rules by sundown tomorrow, if they knew those rules were going to be evenly applied. The problem is not with the students. The problem is getting evenhanded application of the rules from the adults.

The first generation correlate was motivated toward eliminating or driving out undesirable behaviors. If you have a problem with kids fighting with each other, the first thing you have to focus on is driving out the negative. Let's suppose that's where you started your journey, and you have been successful in driving out the negative. The question now turns on what do you substitute for it?

If you don't want students to fight in the school when there is a conflict, what is it you want them to do? That gets us into the second generation, which is to try to create a climate for positive behaviors. If we're going to promote notions of community and cooperation in our schools, one of the things we have to do is put an emphasis on democracy and democratization of the school. We need to have more of the citizens actively involved. Secondary schools that have installed programs in conflict mediation are examples of students taking more responsibility for their own government of behavior and misbehavior.

To create the kind of learning climate where positive behavior and cooperation exist, and people work together effectively, you've got to model it. Teachers have to reflect a more collaborative, empowered workplace, and then model it to the students.

Instructional Leadership

In the effective school, the principal acts as an instructional leader, effectively and efficiently communicating the mission to staff, parents, and students. The principal understands and applies the characteristics of instructional effectiveness in the management of the instructional program.

Leadership is always a very complex issue. If I say we need strong instructional leaders, what image comes to your mind, as a teacher? Do you see a strong leader—an Attila the Hun reincarnated? If you do, you don't have an understanding of what leadership is.

Effective, strong leaders lead through commitment, not through authority. People do not follow effective leaders because they're afraid. People follow effective leaders because they share the vision of the leader.

In the first generation of our work, we focused clearly and almost exclusively on the principal as the instructional leader. We've learned in the second generation that it's still important for the principal to be the instructional leader, but because of the nature of organizational changes going on all around us, the concept of leadership is much more dispersed. The evolution of the role of the principal is now more to become the leader of the leaders, rather than the leader of followers. What we have is collaborative leadership, with teachers becoming more empowered.

Unfortunately, the training principals get through traditional administration programs does not show them how to be leaders of leaders. It shows them how to be managers. People do not need leaders to take them to the place the organization is already headed. Managers will get you there. People need leaders to get to a place they've never been, but really want to go. We're trying to take schools to a place of **Learning for All**, and most schools have not been there yet. We have to reinvent the whole issue of leadership and work hard on it.

High Expectations for Success

In the effective school, there is a climate of high expectations in which the staff believes and demonstrates that all students can attain mastery of the essential school skills. Further, the staff members believe they have the capability to help all students attain that mastery. Embedded in that description are essentially two standards:

1 We believe the kids can learn.

2 We believe that we have the capability, as a faculty and school, to successfully teach all children.

Our work on the first generation correlate of high expectations put a lot of emphasis on the issue of believing in the educability of kids. What we have now learned is high expectations for the learner must be launched from a platform of the teacher first having high expectations for self. It does a teacher very little good to stand up in front of the class and say, "I believe that you can learn. I just don't know how to teach you."

High expectations for self is often referred to in the literature as "teacher sense of efficacy." One of the things the principal must be responsive to and responsible for is keeping track of this sense of efficacy. As we begin to bring changes into a school, we might undermine teacher efficacy or confidence in their own ability to do what's asked of them. When we ask teachers to teach curricular content that's different than they've taught before, they may have doubts in their ability to do that. If we change the math curriculum to a higher order of thinking, putting more emphasis on problem solving and less emphasis on basic arithmetic facts, teachers may not have the confidence to teach that. If we're going into a more hands-on science curriculum, maybe the teacher doesn't know how or have the confidence to work with this. Any time we bring in a change, it may create doubt in the teacher's mind.

A second way to undermine teacher confidence is to change the learners the teacher is being asked to teach. If a teacher has never taught kids who have limited English proficiency, and you start giving that teacher students who come from that background, the teacher may have serious doubts about how to teach those particular kids.

The third way in which we can undermine teacher efficacy or teacher confidence is if we change something in the learning environment. Suppose one Friday, the principal goes into a classroom, hooks up six computers that all network to a computer in the front of the room, and puts a post-it note on the one in front of the room that says, "Start using computers during all of your instruction. I'll be in on Thursday to evaluate your progress."

In this case, we didn't change what is to be learned. We also didn't change anything about the nature of the learners. We did suddenly change the context of the delivery system itself.

It's completely rational for teachers to have doubts about their ability to do what's being asked of them when these changes occur. The principal needs to have strategies in place for dealing with this doubt. Provide your teachers with training and technical assistance around the change. If you're going to ask teachers to teach hands-on science, you'd better provide training and technical assistance for those teachers to become more confident and comfortable with that teaching methodology. If you're asking teachers to teach English as a second language to children, you'd better provide some training and technical assistance for them. If you're going to ask teachers to work with computers in the instructional delivery system in ways they haven't worked with them before, you'd better provide training and technical assistance.

We also need to offer to each teacher models of success. When you bring in change, whether it's content change, learner change, or context change, show teachers places where other teachers have been successful in meeting that change. Show them videos of the change process being played out in other schools or let teachers visit schools that have successfully done some of these things. Efforts to give examples of how it looks in the real world when the change process has been successfully implemented help teachers deal with their own doubts. They will go away understanding, first of all, what it is they have to do differently. They'll also come to the realization that, in most cases, they are able and capable of managing that kind of change.

If you don't have a clear vision of what it looks like on the other side of the change that's being offered, the demons of the change process begin to get very, very large. People get intimidated and begin to believe they can't do it. They begin to stonewall and lose confidence. It's critical to create networks of support to allow and encourage teachers to come together to talk about the good, the bad, and the ugly of the innovation you're trying to implement in your school. If you know schools, you know that teachers spend very little time talking with other teachers right now about good practice. When you create a change effort, you'd better create an environment where they can come together and say, "You know, I'm not having good success with this. This is giving me all kinds of trouble and it's not working for me."

It has to be a safe environment, so when they do come forward, they're not going to feel put down, chastised, or somehow penalized. In the first generation, we put a great emphasis on trying to get teachers to behave in the ways they needed to in order to manifest high expectations for learners. There is a lot of good research out there on how that can happen.

During the second generation, we have to look more at organizational behaviors and not just at what individual teachers can do in their classrooms working alone. What happens when students do not learn? Does the teacher essentially go on to the next lesson anyway? If so, I'm going to conclude that your school never expected all kids to learn in the first place. Even if they did, they failed to set up any system for dealing with kids who didn't learn it the first time.

If you know human behavior and you know that you're not going to be able to teach all kids successfully on one pass, and you're into the mission of **Learning for All**, you're going to have to develop an organizational capability to take the kids who failed to get it the first time to success the next time(s). Schools are going to have to become more collaborative, team-oriented, and community-oriented. Schools are going to have to manifest and create a culture with a high sense of efficacy. Schools are going to have to tell parents, students, and all teachers that we believe all kids can learn and we expect all teachers to teach so all kids do learn.

Frequent Monitoring of Student Progress

In the effective school, student academic progress is measured frequently using a variety of assessment procedures. The results of assessments are used to improve individual student performance and the instructional program.

In the first generation, we put a major emphasis on teachers frequently monitoring student learning and student performance, and adjusting their teaching as a result of this. That's still a very critical core component, but when we go on to the second generation, we now have technology—computers and software systems, the Internet, and more. What we can do is to create a situation which encourages students to self-monitor and to self-correct. Ultimately, that's what adult life is about—being reflective on our own behaviors and, where we see needs or wants, making plans and adjustments. We want to model this behavior first, and teach it second.

One of the questions I'm often asked is, "How frequently should a teacher monitor student progress?"

The answer I always give is, "How prepared is that teacher to adjust instruction?"

If you can adjust every few minutes, monitor every few minutes. If you never adjust what you do based on the facts, why bother monitoring at all?

We're putting much more emphasis on authentic assessments, stressing practical, applied, real-world examples. Also, there has to be a tight alignment between the intended, taught, and assessed curriculum. What we're going to have to do more than we've ever done in the past is become explicit, passionate, and intentional about our educational values.

Clear and Focused Mission

In the U.S., we have chosen over time to use schools to fulfill a lot of social purposes beyond just the learning function. Each of those social purposes is virtuous unto itself. For example, we've asked schools to carefully monitor student inoculations to make sure children are getting the proper protection from childhood diseases. Now that's a worthy goal, but the problem is the more goals you load onto a system, the more difficult it is to keep focused on the core values of the system.

The correlate of clear and focused mission says the primary overarching mission of the school is **Learning for All**. Every other purpose has to be in service to that goal, and we can't let anything distract us from it.

In the first generation, we focused on the mission of teaching for learning for all. I thought I had it right then. I would go all over the country saying, "The mission of your school is teaching for learning for all."

One fateful day I had an "Aha!" reaction as I was flying home from a workshop. I had been uneasy about something for a while and it finally clicked in my head what it was. I had the wrong mission!

When you use the mission statement of teaching for learning for all, you put too much focus on teaching and not enough on learning. The first purpose—the business of a school—is learning, not teaching. We've got to get the focus where it needs to be. By eliminating the words "teaching for," it changes the focus and emphasis, and I hope it makes it easier for all the staff in the school to maintain the needed focus.

Opportunity to Learn and Time on Task

What are some of the implications of this refocus on learning? First of all, schools are going to have to be restructured to assure learning. You cannot get **Learning for All** from a system designed for compulsory attendance with optional learning. It won't work. Second, the curriculum must be raised to a much higher level. There's so much more for kids to know and be able to do in order to be able to succeed in the 21st century workplace and society. Schools are going to have to become comfortable with new ideas—things like visioning, being able to imagine, and beginning with the end in mind.

Again, it's like building a new home. Before you cut one board or turn one shovel of dirt, you've got to be able to envision the end game. You've got to be able to look at the architect's rendering. You've got to be able to translate your values to the architect, so he or she can sketch it out. It's the same thing here. We have to do visioning, backward mapping, and designing from the end game back.

There must also be the ability to do a task analysis, to take the learning goals apart in a way that makes meaningful connections and meaningful bridges to the learners. Providing advanced organizers to give students a model of what a lesson is about, giving immediate feedback, and offering reteaching when needed are all ways to provide those meaningful connections.

In the effective school, teachers allocate significant amounts of instructional classroom time in the essential skills, priorities, and goals. For a high percentage of this time, students are engaged in whole class or larger group, planned, teacher-directed learning activities. One of the things we have to realize is time is one of the major and most important leveraging variables we have to work with in terms of trying to create **Learning for All**.

During the first generation, we emphasized learning of low-level skills. Now we have to put more emphasis on learning the content that is covered rather than just covering content. We have to be much more prudent and strategic in saying what it is that defines the core of essential learning for students. Then we need to match that up with time on task. What we say we care most about is what we must allocate our time, effort, and resources to in our schools.

We're going to have to practice organized abandonment, which simply means we're going to have to let some things go. We can't continue to load more and more on the wagon. Schools only have 15 percent of the time between the child's birth and age 18 to be able to influence the student's whole life. We must become more efficient by abandoning things that are no longer necessary and integrating the curriculum.

We're also going to have to be much more flexible in our time structures. Kids require different amounts of time to learn at comparable levels. We can't hold all kids to the same amount of time. We have to have a system where we can vary the time to meet the needs of the individual.

Home/School Relations

In an effective school, parents understand and support the school's mission, and they're given the opportunity to play important roles in helping the school to achieve this mission. Schools are having to become much more comfortable with this whole issue of parents as partners and parents as teachers.

During the first generation, the role of parents in the education of their children was somewhat unclear. Schools often gave "lip service" to having parents more actively involved in the schooling of their children. However, when pressed, many educators admitted they really did not know how to deal effectively with increased levels of parent involvement in the schools.

In the second generation, the relationship between parents and the school must be an authentic partnership. In the past, when teachers said they wanted more parental involvement, more often than not, they were looking for unqualified support from parents. Many teachers believed that parents, if they truly valued education, knew how to get their children to behave in the ways the school desired.

It is now clear to both teachers and parents that the parent involvement issue is not that simple. Parents are often as perplexed as teachers about the best way to inspire students to learn what the school teaches.

The best hope for effectively confronting the problem—and not each other—is to build enough trust and increased communication to realize both teachers and parents have the same goal.

The effective school correlates, in both their first and second generation forms, drive student learning and performance. There are several measurement instruments available which are useful to assess the perceived presence of the seven correlates in a school, including software such as the *Effective Schools Profiler*™. All schools need to determine where they are on the correlates, and continue to work hard to progress to where they want to be.

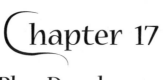

Chapter 17

Plan Development

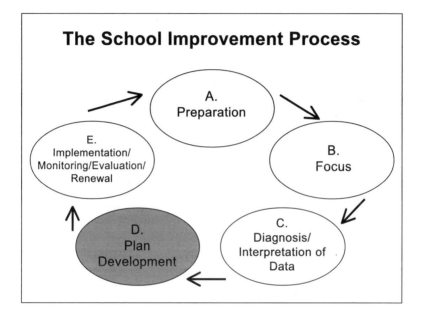

The School Improvement Process

A. Preparation

B. Focus

C. Diagnosis/ Interpretation of Data

D. Plan Development

E. Implementation/ Monitoring/Evaluation/ Renewal

After your team has collected, disaggregated, and analyzed student performance data, you're ready to form the base for specific improvement objectives. These objectives then become the focal point of your school plan.

Improvement objectives should:

- link back to the stated mission which expresses the core values of your school;

- come from a careful analysis of the current student outcome data which determines strengths and weaknesses;

- be stated in terms of student learnings; and

- be reflected, not in a test score, but in a core body of knowledge to be learned.

One way to write improvement objectives is to answer these three questions:

1 Is there a problem?

2 Why might the problem exist?

3 What are the consequences or effects of the problem?

Take each problem statement and turn it into an improvement objective. A well-written improvement objective answers four components: who, does what, when, and how will it be measured? These objectives then form the foundation of your school improvement plan.

A school improvement plan is a theory of cause and effect. It's not an end in itself, but a means to an end. Think of it this way: when you lay out three goals for improvement in your school, those are your "if/ then" statements. If we do this (goal number one) and if we do this (goal number two) and if we do this (goal number three), then student learning performance is going to increase. That's what makes it a theory.

If you see your work as being a theory, then wouldn't it stand to reason that you'd want to have the strongest possible theories? You certainly don't want weak ones. You want a strong, highly probable hypothesis that, if implemented, will make a big difference in the school. What we want to do is go to the knowledge base, see what kind of variables show up in the literature, and determine what will make the biggest difference.

What's the best research to look at? What kind of research should you lean against? There are hundreds of articles that come out in different journals every month. Out of all that mound of information, where do you start to focus your energy?

I would recommend going back to a study done at Harvard a few years ago. Researchers there went out and looked at organizations—not just the schools, but hospitals and private sector companies—all involved in a substantial effort at reform, restructuring, or redesign. They asked these organizations, "What are you actually doing?"

They found two schools of thought. One clustered under innovations or ideas called results-driven interventions. The other clustered under activities-driven interventions.

They found that the results-driven interventions, when implemented and done well, increased productivity dramatically. When they tried to look for the value added by the activities-driven interventions, they couldn't find much of a payoff. It doesn't make it a bad thing to do; just understand that it's not going to have much of a yield.

What are some of the component elements of results-driven interventions or what I call "high-yield strategies?" First of all, a high-yield strategy needs to be knowledge-based. If I was asked to critique your work as a school, in terms of your school improvement plan, one of the things I would ask is, "What research did you lean against to frame these improvement goals?"

If you tell me you just grabbed things out of the air because you thought it was the right thing to do, I'm going to suggest that's a pretty naïve way to build improvement goals in a complex organization like a school. What I would want you to do is link your goals and strategies, wherever appropriate, to the research.

The second criterion by which we ask you to think about your work is the issue of applicability. The profound knowledge must be applicable to schools. The implied contract between us, as you read this, is you have a right, as a practitioner, to believe and expect that I, as an educational writer/consultant, will bring you applicable knowledge that you can actually use in your work. The other part of the social contract that exists between us is I have the right to expect you to take the applicable knowledge and make it actionable in your setting.

You know your setting better than I do. Presumably, I have a better sense of the variables I'm bringing to you. Together, we have a partnership. If we work together and I bring you the concept, and you figure out a way to make it work in your context by making it actionable in your setting, that's the best of all worlds. You see, I can't bring you a finished product.

To use an example, we know that cooperative learning models work. We know there are certain specifications for what ought to go into a good model for cooperative learning. The fact of the matter is, if you go to 10 schools, each one of which is successfully implementing cooperative learning, you'll see some common themes. You'll also see that each one of those schools is different. Their needs are different, their strengths are different, maybe the age of the kids is different, or maybe the subject matter is different. Each school is going to have to make those concepts or principles actionable in different ways.

The third criterion to think about regarding high-yield strategies is they must be results-oriented. We're not going to try to bring you process variables that may be exciting and interesting. One of the worst levels of evidence that I think you can give is that you ought to continue to do whatever you're doing because the kids are happy or the teachers enjoy it.

Don't get me wrong. I'm not opposed to having joyful learners. But one of the other goals that has to go with joyful learning is productive learning. We need instructional strategies and classroom systems that engage kids and keep them positive and excited about what they're doing, but it can't just be all that. It's got to also translate into results.

A study published in *Educational Researcher* years ago looked at a variety of variables to see what added value. For example, the researcher found 152 published studies that looked at the impact of pupil/teacher ratio on measured student performance. Fourteen studies showed that reducing class size resulted in improved student achievement. Thirteen studies showed it has a negative effect and 125 didn't show any significant effects either way.

If you have 152 studies and only 14 show positive effects (the rest show negative or no effects), how do you persuasively argue that reducing class size is a high-yield strategy? There are very few variables in a school that are more expensive to change than pupil/teacher ratio.

We did a rough calculation a few years ago in Michigan, my home state, and discovered if you were to reduce class size by just one student, from whatever it is to one less, it would require enough new money to hire 4,370 new teachers and create 4,370 new classrooms for those teachers to teach in! While it might be attractive to the adults who work in schools to have lower pupil/teacher ratios, you have to be very prudent in weighing out the options.

Out of 69 studies on teacher salary, 54 showed no effect. If the only thing that happened to you tomorrow was your salary went up $25,000, but your knowledge base didn't go up and your support system around that knowledge (the materials your classroom uses, the computers you might have, etc.) stayed the same, the salary increase would be unlikely to produce higher levels of learning.

Some of our favorite variables, the ones we often grab for, are often the most expensive ones and don't seem to have a very high payoff.

Does that mean resources really don't make a difference? I want to say emphatically, "No! Resources do make a difference!" However, you must focus those resources on the factors that make an impact on student performances.

Benjamin Bloom's study, published in 1984, is what I call a "golden oldie." (By the way, principals should ask candidates interviewing for teaching positions if they know anything about Benjamin Bloom and his research. If they haven't been prepared to deal with these kind of studies, I'd be very wary of hiring them.) Bloom searched for methods of group instruction that were as effective as one-to-one instruction. He compared typical classroom learning— 30 students with one teacher teaching a lesson—to students who were individually tutored. How well did the one-to-one group of tutored students look in their achievement on the same lessons as the 30-to-one classroom?

He found that the average score for the one-to-one tutored group was two standard deviations above the mean for the 30-to-one group. If you know anything about probability and statistics, a two standard deviation difference is a profound difference in terms of student learning.

If I went to a private sector organization—Ford Motor Company or General Motors or any large company—and said, "I've got a strategy of production which will raise your productivity the equivalent of two standard deviations," that company would make me the darling of the boardroom and pay me a lot of money for that information!

Even Kuwait, with all of its oil resources, cannot afford a delivery system of education where you have one teacher for every child. Instead, we have to look at some kind of grouping phenomena. The question Bloom then asked was, "Can we get the 30-to-one arrangement to be equal or nearly equal to the tutorial model?"

The answer he came up with was, "Yes, we can!"

What leading indicators or strategies make a difference?

Mastery learning, by itself, will increase student achievement one full standard deviation. To implement mastery learning successfully in a school, however, requires restructuring the school. You can't just do that in one classroom at a time. You've got to set it up on a continuous improvement, continuous learning system—and that's going to require cutting across grade levels and classrooms.

What a payoff, though—one full standard deviation! We can increase productivity by just doing that in our schools. We don't need any more money other than the money that might be needed to provide training to be sure that the teachers know and are comfortable with the mastery learning model. We don't need more people necessarily. This is true of most of the high-yield strategies.

If, every time a teacher steps in front of a group of kids, that teacher can be confident the students have met the prerequisites for what he or she is about to teach, that will, in and of itself, move the group up by .7 of a standard deviation. Again, that's a profound effect.

Most teachers agree that there are significant differences in rates of learning. If you look at a classroom, some kids seem to get it right away, other kids get it very slowly, and some don't get it at all. You might inadvertently conclude these kids are learning at different rates. What Bloom found, however, was most (but not all) of those perceived differences in learning rates are really a function of the presence or absence of prerequisites. The kids who tend to get the new concept quickly are the ones who had learned what it was they needed to know. They're ready to meet that new learning. The kids who are struggling are the ones who didn't learn the prerequisites in the first place. Now you've added the additional complexity of not knowing what they needed to know on top of the new knowledge and it just becomes a buzzing confusion. As you look at those kids over time, they keep falling further and further behind.

If we had a system that was mastery-learning-oriented and assured that kids didn't move to the next levels of learning until they had met the prerequisites for what they needed to know, we would see significant improvement right there. If you do these two things, you can get about a one-and-a-half standard deviation improvement!

You can begin to realize half a gain in standard deviation by just working with parents and increasing parent involvement in some of the things you're trying to do. Parents and teachers make powerful partners.

These strategies are not all additive. You don't just add 1 plus .7 plus .5 and get things to work. They're not that totally independent. But picking a high-yield strategy, backed by the research, and carefully and thoughtfully implementing it, will go a long way toward enhancing student achievement.

Another study by Philip A. Griswold, Kathleen J. Cotton, and Joe B. Hansen reviewed effective educational practices in compensatory education programs. The organizational attributes they found included positive school and classroom climate; clear project goals and objectives; coordination with a regular program; parent and community involvement; professional development and training; evaluation of results; and strong leadership. The instructional attributes they found included appropriate instructional materials, methods, and approaches; maximum use of academic learning time; high expectations for students; regular feedback and reinforcement; closely monitored student progress; and rewarding and recognizing excellence. It wouldn't take a lot of interpretation to link these variables back to the seven correlates of effective schools!

I'm not suggesting that a school, in the name of improvement, take on all of these at once. What I would like to recommend is that, after careful consideration, a school's leadership team should bite off the chunk it feels it can handle. If the team believes it can only work on expectations or wants to spend a significant amount of time next year working on feedback, reinforcement, and rewards systems, let that be the focus.

I believe, and my experience so far tells me, if we can get a school to do a few things and do them with fidelity and with some depth, we're going to get a higher yield than if we scramble 1,000 different ideas.

Another major piece of work, by Herb Walberg, my friend and colleague, talks about productive teaching and instruction. Every four or five years, he goes back and does a "what's new" in the knowledge base, looking at it in levels. In the first level are methods and patterns of teaching that a single teacher can accomplish without unusual arrangements or equipment. His high-yield strategies include increasing engagement rates of students through more active participation; giving corrective feedback in a timely fashion; providing reinforcements and incentives; explicitly teaching what it is you want kids to know; and comprehensive teaching.

In other words, what he's talking about first doesn't even require school-wide participation. It doesn't even require that all teachers at a given grade level participate. I, as an individual teacher, could go into my classroom and do these things alone.

Obviously, I would encourage you not to constrain it to a single teacher, but rather think through these ideas in a comprehensive way and select some for your school.

Walberg's second level requires some special planning, student grouping, or materials. These high-yield strategies include programmed instruction; mastery learning; adaptive instruction; and assisted or technology-assisted learning.

His Level 3 strategies talk about effects that are unique to particular methods of teaching. High-yield strategies in reading include adaptive speed or deliberately working on helping kids to pick up their pace when they read; the phonics-based approach, which has been one of those controversial ones, but has a good history of evidence behind it; and pictures in the text to give meaning that makes it easier for kids to "hook on."

In the area of writing, he talks about inquiry methods, where kids are given major projects and can go on the Internet to dig out information; specific questions; free writing; and working on grammar and mechanics. If you're going to help kids to be the best writers they can be, they need to have that sense of grammar and mechanics. The earlier kids learn these things, the more they will become enabling tools rather than something that has to be so directly focused.

In the area of science, Walberg again points to inquiry teaching; audio tutorials; and original source papers. Thanks to the Internet, kids will be able to get a lot closer to the original manuscripts or the original authors. Some of these scholars are even doing chat rooms where the kids can interact. There's a whole new frontier being opened up right now!

In the area of math, he focuses on manipulatives; problem solving; and, testing on what's taught. If you want to look bad, just teach kids one thing and test them on another.

Level 4 effects are unique to special students or techniques. They include early intervention; preschool programs; cross-age tutoring; and psycholinguistic training.

One of the things that I'd like to encourage you to do, as a team and as a faculty, is go through this chapter again. Set up small study groups of two or three people with the task of exploring one of these variables. Then come back and share your findings— not for the purpose of saying one wins and one loses. Instead, let's see if you can find the common ground and pick off a few variables that your team truly believes in after reading about them.

Take the research from where you are, and take your school from where it is, and help each other grow to the next level. Challenge yourself, in the best sense of professional challenge, to be the very best educator you can possibly be in the very best school that can possibly be.

If you do that, and look at the research in a serious way, significant amounts of new resources from the outside are not necessarily going to be the tradition that you need. You can develop a plan for your school that works, because you are the best people to deliver those goals and that improvement.

Chapter 18

Making it Happen

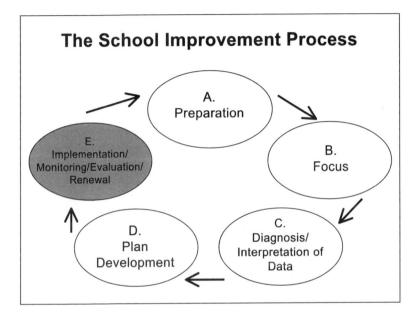

The School Improvement Process

A. Preparation

B. Focus

C. Diagnosis/ Interpretation of Data

D. Plan Development

E. Implementation/ Monitoring/Evaluation/ Renewal

Implementation strategies require a common language of improvement. Teaching the common language—one in which everyone understands the terminology and can communicate freely—isn't a "do-it-once-and-forget-it" proposition. To maintain the focus, the common language must be renewed and revisited regularly.

Time to implement the plan is also critical. There are lots of ways a school can find the necessary time—before- or after-school meetings, release time provided by substitutes, extended lunch hours with teachers alternating covering one period, compensated time when school is not in session, etc.

You get the idea. The important thing is to find the time!

The improvement process must also become standard operating procedure or part of the school culture. It should be ongoing and self-renewing.

I would like to recommend to schools, as they think about school improvement and school-based planning, that they set three major goals and no more than three. After all, a school can't take on everything at once. It's important to focus on the big ideas. Unlike private sector business, we can't shut down, do a model changeover, and then have a grand reopening. We have to do it on the fly, so to speak!

Big Ideas

There are a few improvement goals I call "big ideas" because of the major impact they can have. One of those big ideas is in the area of **curriculum alignment**. Teachers have got to come to believe in their heads, their hearts, and their guts that, if they teach the intended curriculum that they have been given by their school district, and the students master that curriculum, the students will do well on whatever measurements and assessments the district and state require from them.

I put curriculum alignment at the top of my list of things that schools need to take on because there are moral issues involved. I'm going to use some harsh words just to make my point. When the adults in a school or school district are negligent around curriculum alignment, who pays the price? The students! How do you morally justify asking your students to pay for your adult negligence as teachers and administrators? I think that's a hard moral position to take.

Let me go one level deeper. It's not all students paying equally for adult negligence. Some subsets of your students pay a greater price for your negligence than others. Guess who gets to pay the greatest price for adult negligence around curriculum alignment? Those students most dependent on the school as their sole source of academic learning—namely, the disadvantaged children in your school! How, as adults, teachers, and administrators, do you morally justify and rationalize asking the most needy children in your school to pay the greatest price for your negligence around issues of curriculum alignment?

Another reason why I think curriculum alignment ought to go at the top of the list is based on what I have found through my work with various schools around the country. Others have found similar results. If a school is willing to take careful steps to make sure there's a good alignment between the intended, taught, and assessed curriculum, that school can anticipate about a 25 percent to 30 percent increase in student achievement and student learning. That's a huge increase! Why would any school want to ignore that possibility? Why would any faculty want to ignore the notion that, if they do these things (which I think are the morally right things to do in the first place), the payoff is they will see huge bumps in student achievement for all students, but most particularly for those who are most dependent on the school as their source of academic learning?

A third reason for putting curriculum alignment at the top of the list has to do with the fact that virtually any other innovation that you bring into your school for the purpose of trying to improve student learning as evidenced through assessments of one sort or another assumes that there is good alignment between the intended, taught, and tested curriculum.

We need three things to achieve curriculum alignment, each one of which is important:

1 We need to have clear curricular goals. We want to be able to answer, with specificity, what it is we want the kids to know, do, and be disposed to do at the end of the day, the year, and at the end of their experience in our school. We need to answer this before we even begin the journey.

2 We need to develop core curricular models. Many states are doing this. Once the goals have been specified, we need to translate and interpret them through a series of courses, programs, and learning experiences for kids. You can't teach at the level of general goal statements. You've got to operationalize them into specific instructional objectives, learning tasks, and classroom activities.

3 We need an assessment system that makes sense. How will we be able to determine that students know, do, and are disposed to do what we set out to teach?

Schools must become much more intentional in deciding what's worth knowing in the world, what they're going to emphasize, how they're going to deliver that instruction, and what they're going to use to assess learning.

A study done a few years ago at Michigan State University proved to be a profound insight for me. The research team asked a simple question "Do all standardized, norm-referenced, commercially available tests on the market essentially measure the same fourth grade mathematics content?"

Maybe as we get further into the math hierarchy, we might find more variability, but at fourth grade, it seems to me we're still pretty close to the basics. My assumption was that probably all of the commercially available norm-referenced tests measure essentially the same content, so I would have answered "yes" to the researchers' question.

The research team developed a way of classifying the tasks in the tests, sorting items just like you might sort mail. Out of many tests, they found two had the most overlap in content. However, those two tests had an overlap in only about 30 percent of the items. The other 70 percent was unique to each test.

One of the tests required the students to have prior knowledge about working with graphs and charts—in fact, 25 percent of the items assumed this knowledge. In other words, one item out of every four assumed that the children had working knowledge with graphs and charts.

Well, I'm here to tell you, if you have a curricular and instructional program that does not emphasize graphs and charts in the K-4 years, and you give your students a nationally-normed test where one out of every four items presumes comprehensive knowledge of working with graphs and charts, your school and your teachers are going to look bad!

The researchers also noticed that one of the commercially available tests at the time had four items on it that had to do with Roman numerals. They were able to show that, if two students took that test and scored exactly the same on all the other items, but one student got the four Roman numeral items right and the other student got them wrong, it could translate out to as much as two full grade equivalence differences on that test!

I have two grown sons who are now on their own, but I'm here to bear witness to the fact that, if my boys know anything about Roman numerals, they learned it at school. I cannot remember one conversation we had at the family dinner table when those boys were growing up that ever included Roman numerals! If you're going to use a test with that much weight on something like Roman numerals, you cannot leave to chance the curricular and instructional component that requires and compels teachers to teach at least those minimum concepts around Roman numerals.

To make a serious commitment to the broad goal area of aligning intended, taught, and assessed curriculum is about a two- to three-year effort. It requires a lot of thought, careful planning, and work to fully implement this whole issue of instructional alignment. Why should you engage that much time and effort? The payoff is increased student achievement, along with a clear understanding of what in your school is working or not working.

One of the most obvious leading indicators that a school has at its disposal is **how it chooses to use time**. A study by Lorin W. Anderson and Herb Walberg, *Timepiece: Extending and Enhancing Learning Time*, gives you some benchmarks against which to begin to look at your own school and make some judgments. They start with the concept of allocated time, which simply means the time, in the broadest sense, that a school has to work with in terms of student learning and student performance.

The easiest way to determine allocated time for your school would be to take the length of the school day and multiply it by the number of days your school is supposed to be in session. If your school is in session six hours a day for 180 days, multiply 6 by 180 to get the allocated time you have to work with in terms of instruction.

Now how does the time get spent? One of the first questions asked in the research was, "Of all the allocated time of schools in the U.S., what percentage is devoted to instruction?"

The researchers found that only about 83 percent of allocated time is actually devoted to instruction in the typical U.S. school. That means that, somewhere along the line, we're losing about 17 percent of our allocated time. It might be spent on pep rallies, assemblies, or other things that draw us away from curriculum and instructional emphasis.

Collect your data (and that's always what I ask!) and find out if your school is typical in this regard. Let's assume, for purposes of discussion, that it is and you're losing about 17 percent of instructional time. One of the things you can then ask is, "What could be done to cut that loss?"

I don't believe a typical school in America can go to zero on slippage between instructional time and allocated time. That's unrealistic. There are real things that intrude on the school that cannot be ignored. There is definitely a place for pep rallies, assemblies, and other events. However, perhaps one of the things you can try to do as part of your overall school improvement plan is say, "We're going to take that 17 percent loss and try to cut it close to half. Our goal is to reduce that loss between allocated and instructional time to about nine percent."

If you had a 200-day school year and you were to cut the loss from 17 percent to about nine percent, you would have saved the equivalent of almost 18 days of instruction that could be deployed for learning goals.

You might ask, "What are the things that intrude on our learning time and how can we manage some of those?"

That might mean making some hard decisions.

Anderson and Walberg also talked about time on task. They asked, "When students are in the classroom, how much of the time are they actually engaged in instruction?"

They found that only about 62 percent of allocated time was spent with the kids engaged in instruction. In Japan, when you use the same definition of time on task and you look at their classrooms, their time-on-task rates run at about 90 percent. It's quite a difference from ours! When you translate that down, it's saying that, in a Japanese classroom, out of a 60-minute class period, the kids are on task about 54 minutes. In the U.S. classroom, our kids are only on task about 37 minutes out of 60. The difference between 54 minutes and 37 minutes may not seem like a lot until you begin to recognize that we're talking about every hour of every day of every year that kids are in school. Inching up the time on task allows more leverage to improve student learning and performance.

When students are in class and they're not on task learning, what are they most frequently found to be doing? Often, teachers will say, "Well, they're probably fooling around, talking to their neighbors, or misbehaving."

Again, you have to look at the data. The research shows that the most frequent thing students are doing when they're in class, but not on task learning, is waiting for the teacher. The teacher is in the front of the room, working up a sweat, trying to collect all the lunch money, collect late homework assignments, give out information, do this, do that—the teacher's active, no doubt about it! But remember, you've got 25, 28, or 30 kids sitting there, watching this.

One of my colleagues, who does a lot of public speaking on school reform, says if an alien came from another planet, hovered around a public school, and went back to the home planet to describe what a public school was all about, the alien might say, "A school is a place where young people go to watch old people work."

The final characterization that the Anderson and Walberg study takes up is the issue of academic learning time or the amount of time that kids are on task in classrooms learning those things that the school says it cares most about. They discovered it is only about 42 percent of the time. Students in high schools in the U.S. spend only 55 percent as much time on task learning academic subjects as compared to students in high schools in Japan.

I'm not a big fan of cross-cultural comparisons because they can be very misleading, but the point I'm trying to make is, if you have your kids working half as hard, putting in half as much time and effort learning something as Japanese students, your pedagogy better be darn good to offest that differential in time and effort!

Back in 1977, the National Science Foundation funded a grant which required K-3 teachers across the U.S. to indicate how much time and effort they spent on science, social studies, math, and reading.

They were spending about 18 minutes a day in science, about 21 minutes in social studies, 42 minutes in math, and 97 minutes in reading.

Along came the *Nation At Risk* report in the early 1980's and, with it, the call for school reform. One of the rallying cries was to put more emphasis on math and science in our schools, from kindergarten all the way through 12th grade. In 1986, the National Science Foundation funded another grant to see how time allocations may have changed in the primary grades in this country. The President, governors, university scholars, and business leaders were all asking for more emphasis on math and science. All of these forces were operating together to say, "We've got to do a better job of teaching our kids important concepts in math and science!"

Look at how much change happened in that time:

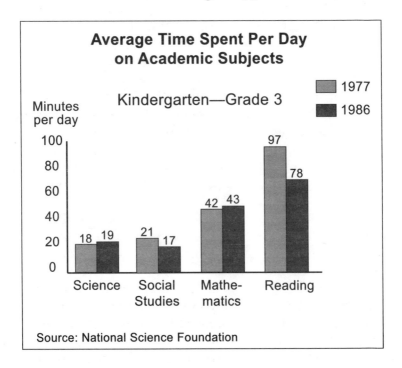

Average Time Spent Per Day on Academic Subjects

Kindergarten—Grade 3

Minutes per day

Source: National Science Foundation

Science went from 18 minutes a day to 19, social studies went from 21 to 17, math went up by one minute, and reading went from 97 down to 78 minutes. The conclusion you have to come to is, if there has been a change in reform around science and math, it has been kept a secret from the K-3 teachers! It obviously hasn't changed their priorities.

You may say, "Well, that's the primary grades. It's different in higher elementary grades."

The same question was asked of fourth through sixth grade teachers:

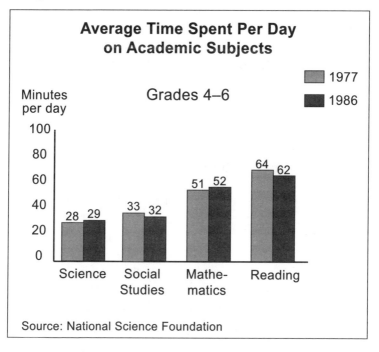

As in the early grades, there was very little change. The same is true for middle schools. Ask how much longer the middle school math course is now than it was in 1977, and you'll be told not much or not at all. If you're a high school teacher, how much longer is 9th grade math now than it was 15 or 20 years ago? Odds are, it hasn't changed much, either.

The first signal we can bank on that we have seriously made a change in the model that we are trying to deliver to kids is going to be in terms of time allocations. When we see time for math going up, even if it means time for something else is going down, we can legitimately begin to believe, anticipate, and predict that there are going to be significant changes in outcomes in math. If we leave time the same, even if we get a little bit better at our instruction, the value added is probably going to be minimal.

Look at the data on the graph for the early grades. Notice the relationship in time between science and reading. Science is at about 20 minutes a day and reading is at about 80 minutes. There's a four-to-one ratio of time allocation in the primary grades between science and reading.

Now look at the chart for grades four through six. Science is at about 30 minutes and reading is at about 60 minutes. In others words, we're putting in twice as much time and effort in reading in grades 4 through 6 as in science, or a two-to-one ratio.

Think about these differences in allocation and see if you can discover a great truth about what's going on here. In the U.S., up until very recently, when we did cross-cultural comparisons with other industrialized countries of the world, our students tended to score near the bottom of the list with respect to science achievement. On the other hand, in 1993, when the U.S. Office of Education released a cross-cultural study that compared our kids with kids in other developed countries in the world relative to reading, our kids scored near the top.

Do you get any notions, from looking at these data, as to what may explain why our kids do as poorly as they do in science and so much better relative to other countries in reading? Do you think it might have anything to do with time on task?

I'm certainly not saying we should spend less time on reading. What I am saying, though, is if I had my "druthers," I would require every school to start, as its first major improvement reform goal, to take on the issues of alignment between the intended, taught, and assessed curriculum in a very serious way—and that includes taking a serious look at how time is being spent.

There has to be a more effective way to **structure the classroom**. Once you change the function or mission of the system, you have to change the form that delivers that function. I know that sounds like a lot of abstract concepts and words, but let me try to drive home the point about the structure of the system. Here are three questions that I have asked educators to vote on:

 How many of you believe that, when kids show up for the first day of their experience in the public system, they already reflect variability in readiness for what the school has to teach them?

How many of you believe, from your experiences as teachers and administrators, that kids learn at different rates?

3 How many of you believe that what kids learn in one grade is somewhat dependent on what they did or did not learn in previous grades?

When I take a vote on these three questions and put the results of that vote together, here's what I can say. Most educators believe there is variability in readiness for learning when children enter the system. Most educators believe there is variability in rates of learning as children move through the system. Most educators believe there is dependency across the levels of learning in the system—or what we do builds on what's gone before.

Based on that consensus, there is no way to deliver the **Learning for All** mission in a system that is age- and grade-based. Why would you put all the kids who reflect a wide range of readiness for learning in the same learning group simply because they're all five years of age? It might make sense to put all kids who are five years old together if your goal is to keep attendance because it's easier to take attendance if everybody in the room is close in height. If your goal is learning, though, placing kids on the basis of chronological age makes no sense. Wouldn't you want to take the kids who are at different points on the learning continuum and put each one in a learning setting tailored more for them, where the curriculum is set to challenge them and move them forward?

Old classroom structures designed for compulsory attendance must give way to new classroom structures if we're going to make significant progress toward the **Learning for All** mission. The only way public schools are going to be more successful than they are is to go to a concept I call customized service. You've got to vary the system to meet the needs of the learners. Once you start doing that, the old structures, the age-grade-based structures, are going to have to give way.

We need to build a system based on **ungraded, continuous progress, flexibly scheduled schools.** That does not mean we are going to track kids. Rather, we need to place them in achievement-centered groups—not ability groups. A child might be in one achievement-centered group for mathematics, another one for reading, a different one for science, and so on. We're going to place them where they can be appropriately challenged in the curriculum and where they can succeed. We're going to abandon grade levels to move along in a continuous progress way. Since we don't need to keep every child in the same reading group or science group or other learning group for a whole year, kids can move through the system as quickly as they need to in order to take advantages of their different rates of learning.

Block scheduling is a concept that has been used at all levels. It's a way of trying to repackage time to make better use of it. With bigger blocks of time, kids and teachers can dig into subjects in a deeper way. One of the criticisms of the 50-minute period in high school science, for example, is as soon as students get the lab equipment out on the table to do the experiment, it's time to clean up. They can't really dig into the topic with the depth they need to learn it. Creating a block schedule, which might go to a double period or even a triple period in science, allows more study, more guided practice, and so on.

The **year-round school** concept is growing in popularity. Here's the logic behind it. There is no industry in the U.S. that could stay in business by having its physical plant shut down 25 percent of the time. We have a multibillion-dollar industry called public schools on a September-to-June model, letting it sit idle in the summer.

It makes no sense if our mission is learning. There is no evidence that the human brain is unable to learn in the summer! There is no evidence that most of the kids have to be on the family farm to work in the summer.

We already own the buses. We already own the buildings. We already own the books, computers, and other materials. Why can't we put the pieces together and extend the opportunity for learning?

We have learned so much about **the brain and how it functions** relative to human learning and human performance in the last 10 or 15 years that for any teacher or administrator to ignore that research is downright unprofessional. The brain researchers make it pretty clear: if you want kids to retain what it is they're learning, they've got to be able to make a meaningful connection between the new material and what they've learned before.

Task analysis is one way to make that connection, by breaking down what it is we want kids to know and then connecting it to what they already know. **Reciprocal teaching** is another way to connect. One of the key differences between good adult readers and poor adult readers is that the good readers have the capacity, inclination, and natural notion to develop **advanced organizers**. They've developed a theory ahead of time based on the title of what they're about to read. Then, as they read the material, they're able to modify, adjust, and refine their theory, so it makes it a lot easier to comprehend what they're reading. Poor adult readers, for the most part, do not tend to develop those theories of what it is they're about to do. They spend so much time encoding the material that they can't remember what they've read. If you're serious about literacy, and you're not satisfied with the results you're getting, look at the research around reciprocal teaching and advanced organizers.

Another brain research concept that is critical to all of this is the issue of **immediate feedback**. One of the things we know from the brain research is that the human brain benefits a lot from immediate feedback. If it acts, and then connects consequences to the action, it can modify its learning very quickly.

One of the problems you have in schools, and here's another place where technology can help us, is that teachers cannot be there, on site, for 28 kids to give them all immediate feedback at the appropriate stroke in the teaching/learning process. We're looking at ways to begin to use computers in instruction to advance learning as an end to itself. One of the things you want to look at is how we can equip hardware and software to be able to provide students with immediate feedback.

Yet another concept that is strongly supported now by the research is **reteaching**. If a school was able to organize itself to take those students who didn't learn the lesson on the first go-around and get them back through for one loop of reteaching, they could anticipate about a 25 percent bump up in student achievement.

Other big ideas include **cooperative learning, cross-age tutoring, student-led parent teacher conferences**, and **schools as learning communities**. Involving senior citizens as tutors, sort of like academic foster parents, has been shown to be very successful in many communities. Business partnerships, including working in apprenticeship models where part of the learning actually occurs outside of the school in real work settings, represent another growing area.

We've only begun to scratch the surface on this. The strategies I've suggested here are by no means the only ones. They are intended to suggest what schools can do if all members are willing to dedicate themselves to the new mission and draw upon the existing knowledge base to guide the change process in their school and classroom.

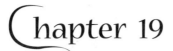hapter 19

Continuous School Improvement

It's hard to believe, but it's been more than 30 years since the first journal articles reporting the findings of what was to become known as the effective schools research were published. These studies were seen as radical and greeted with great skepticism.

The establishment voices in public education, especially the university-based researchers, were heard raising such questions as, "What do you mean all students can learn? Do you really believe that schools can and should be held accountable for student achievement? Do you really believe that schools control enough of the critical variables to assure that all students do learn?"

Given the current policy environment, these questions are no longer even asked. My, how times have changed!

Now, we have whole states holding individual schools accountable for student achievement, usually as measured by various state-sponsored assessments. We have the President of the United States outlawing social promotions. We have advocates of school choice, charter schools, and even vouchers demanding that schools assure student learning or be closed down.

Today, no one seems to doubt that schools can and do make a difference. Some policymakers have gone so far as to say, or at least imply, that schools make all the difference when it comes to student learning and student achievement.

The effective schools research represented a vision of what was possible when it came to student learning and student achievement. The massive changes in the world brought about by the technology revolution and global competition served to propel the necessity for deep and sustained school change. The confluence of the effective schools research and the changing world has launched an unprecedented demand for reform of public schools.

Public schools may be quickly running out of time. Advocates of alternative forms of schooling suggest that the schools have less than a decade to make the necessary changes or they will be out of business. Goodness knows, many schools have tried to reform themselves; some have even been successful. Unfortunately, many that have tried have failed for one reason or another, and still many more have not even tried. They seem to believe that this clarion call for fundamental reform will pass, as has been true so often in the past.

In many ways, this concept of returning to the knowledge base of teaching and learning, and curriculum and instruction, to find answers to student learning problems seems strange, almost bizarre. After all, the prevailing notion was that learning problems were internal to the learner and controlled by nonschool factors, such as home and family background. Teachers and principals were often dumbfounded when told that their school plan was a theory. They had trouble seeing a goal in the school plan as a working cause-and-effect hypothesis, but, in fact, this description was accurate. It helped many school teams reformulate the mental models they had been using to guide the planning process.

Once the cause-and-effect relationships that produce student learning have been presented, most educators indicate that it seems obvious to them. So what's the problem? Why don't or can't schools easily adopt the continuous improvement model?

The best hope for schools is to be found in the fundamental principles of the continuous improvement model. The principles are based on certain assumptions and beliefs. The overriding question centers itself around whether or not schools meet these assumptions:

Continuous improvement works with complex systems.

I believe that schools clearly qualify as complex, goal-oriented, resource-limited, people-driven systems. Schools meet this requirement for a systems approach to continuous improvement. The profound knowledge coming from the school and teacher effectiveness research of the last quarter century affirms the complex nature of the school and classroom. No one today would seriously challenge the assumption that schools are complex systems.

Effective systems require a clear aim.

The aim of public education is changing and becoming clearer at the same time. If you were to study the actions of state and federal policymakers, it would be clear that the aim of public education is fast becoming compulsory **Learning for All**. On the other hand, if you were to study the proceedings of most local school board meetings or teacher and administrator association meetings, it would not be at all clear that the first purpose of the school is successful **Learning for All**. Even the parent groups have not come to grips with the fact that the mission is changing. Parents, as well as others, still cling to the notion that the structure and functioning of the school can remain the same.

Unlike many of the other countries to whom the United States is often compared and found wanting when it comes to the education of children, we have chosen to use schools as social instruments for many other social "goods" beyond learning. Schools have been used as a primary instrument for overcoming segregation in the larger society and its many institutions. Schools are expected to be transportation systems. Schools are expected to provide food, entertainment, and so on. Make no mistake: these are all important social functions. The problem for schools is one of goal displacement or at least goal diffusion. It's difficult to keep your eye on **the** ball when many balls are coming at you all at once!

Complex systems must be able to manage their aim.

The greatest challenge facing the schools on the journey to continuous school improvement is their current inability to manage the learning mission. Remember, until fairly recently, schools were held accountable for inputs and maybe some processes. Schools were not held accountable for outputs or results, especially results that purport to reflect student learning and student performance. The vast majority of schools and districts in the United States today can manage the mission of compulsory attendance with optional learning. The fact that they can manage the attendance mission suggests that, once the new mission is accepted, they will develop systems for managing learning. Unfortunately, if we don't find a way to assist the schools with this instructional management task, it may be too late.

Complex systems must have a pervasive commitment to the mission.

A shared sense of mission needs to occur at many levels of the public education system. The effective schools research has known for a long time that one of the keys to the effective school is this strong sense of mission evidenced across the faculty and staff of the school. In addition, the school district personnel must also share the same levels of passion and be there to support the individual schools as they strive to reach the goal of **Learning for All**.

Unfortunately, this standard is rarely met by most school districts. It seems that many people in central office have come to believe that the system exists to serve their special function and not the learning function. Above the school district level, any consensus as to the primary mission of public education further breaks down. For example, teacher preparation programs oftentimes seem indifferent to schools as they attempt to describe the kind of teacher needed for today's schools.

Quality systems focus on prevention.

The cheapest way to solve a problem is to prevent it in the first place. Quality organizations build a culture of prevention. Schools have little history in attempting to solve a learning problem by preventing it in the first place. We say that we can't predict problems the same way that a manufacturing company might because we are dealing with human beings. This assumption must be challenged. If you ask experienced teachers what problems they anticipate facing when a new school year begins, they can tell you. Unfortunately, the system is not designed to prevent problems, so there is little interest in asking teachers such questions. After all, what would the system do with the information?

Quality systems solve problems when they occur.

Ideally, a quality system strives to prevent problems from ever occurring. Unfortunately, this is nearly impossible, so we need to be strongly committed to solving the unavoidable problems when they occur. If students are placed in the wrong learning group, given their current level of skills, they should be reassigned as soon as the problem is recognized. How does it make any sense to allow a student to linger in failure and frustration for any length of time?

We now know what the problems are. We know what needs to change in order to solve those problems. The basic framework for an action plan to solve those problems has been articulated. The rest is up to us. Do we have the will to make the journey?

Chapter 20

Process Recommendations

I would like to conclude with some process recommendations that I strongly believe could make a huge difference in public education:

Process Recommendation #1: The United States needs a national, state, and local set of strategies that will cause all the stakeholders to accept the new mission and embrace the changes that will be required in order to assure successful **Learning for All**. With the crisis in educational leadership that is becoming more apparent each day, we need to provide effective, change-oriented leaders and give them job security, especially at the local level, or we'll never see the sustainable changes in the schools.

Process Recommendation #2: In order to preserve the cherished state control of public education and stay in keeping with the U. S. Constitution, each state should develop an instructional management system and make it available at no cost to each district and school in its jurisdiction. The instructional management system should incorporate cutting-edge information technologies, and should be accompanied by the needed training and technical assistance to insure quick and appropriate adoption of the system at the local level. In fact, I believe the first state in the union that is able to develop and deploy such a system will leapfrog ahead of the other states on the journey to school reform.

The development and implementation of the instructional management system is costly and time-consuming, and should not be left to each district to reinvent the system one district at a time. The system should be flexible enough to allow local districts to add local priorities to the state's priorities, preserving the flavor of local district control.

Process Recommendation #3: Our nation and each individual state need to engage in "operation consensus" to get all the stakeholders on the same track when it comes to the mission of public education. In addition, to the extent possible, operation consensus should try to build agreement on the best practices for achieving the mission of **Learning for All**. Many local conflicts come as a result of a lack of understanding or commitment to the research evidence that can be assembled to support a best practice.

Process Recommendation #4: The effective schools research model has always advocated that schools begin with the end in mind and design down. This strategy can work just as well in trying to prevent learning problems before they occur. If schools, districts, and states were to isolate the factors that are associated with success and failure, they would find the early alert signals and then respond appropriately.

For example, if students must pass a high school proficiency examination in order to receive a recognized diploma, one could ask how many students in the current system can meet this standard if they can't read. If we find the answer to be "very few," then the schools can start to customize or differentiate service as soon as the earliest literacy problems begin to appear.

Process Recommendation #5: Schools need to develop feedback systems that will provide evidence of student learning problems at the earliest possible moment. In the past, schools didn't concern themselves much with this problem since learning was optional. However, now that the new mission and heightened levels of accountability are upon the schools, they need to act much sooner to solve learning problems.

The journey to continuous school improvement is beckoning. Let's get on the right path!

Bibliography

Ackoff, Russell L., *Creating the Corporate Future*. John Wiley & Sons, Inc., New York, NY, 1981.

Anderson, Lorin W. and Herbert J. Walberg, *Timepiece: Extending and Enhancing Learning Time*. NASSP, Reston, VA, 1993.

Argyris, Chris, *Knowledge for Action: A Guide to Overcoming Barriers to Organizational Change*. Jossey-Bass Inc., San Francisco, CA, 1993.

Bloom, Benjamin, S., "The Search for Methods of Group Instruction as Effective as One-to-One Instruction," *Educational Leadership*, May 1984.

Brookover, Wilbur B., Fritz A. Erickson, and Alan W. McEvoy, *Creating Effective Schools: An In-service Program for Enhancing School Learning Climate and Achievement*. Revised Edition, Learning Publications, Holmes Beach, FL, 1996.

Business Week, "Needed: Human Capital," Sept. 19, 1988.

Canady, Robert Lynn and Michael D. Rettig, *Block Scheduling: A Catalyst For Change in High Schools*. Eye on Education, Inc., Princeton, NJ, 1995.

Deming, W. Edwards, *The New Economics For Industry, Government, and Education*. Massachusetts Institute of Technology, Center for Advanced Engineering Study, Cambridge, MA, 1989.

Dolan, W. Patrick, *Restructuring Our Schools: A Primer on Systemic Change*. Systems and Organizations, Kansas City, MO, 1994.

Edmonds, Ronald, "Effective Schools for the Urban Poor," *Educational Leadership*, October 1979.

Gagne, Robert M., *Conditions of Learning*. Holt, Rinehart & Winston, Inc., New York, NY, 1965.

Griswold, Philip A., Kathleen J. Cotton, and Joe B. Hansen, *Effective Compensatory Education Source Book Volume 1: A Review of Effective Educational Practices.* Superintendent of Documents, U.S. Government Printing Office, Washington, D.C.

Hanushek, Eric A., "The Impact of Differential Expenditures on School Performance," *Educational Researcher*, May 1989.

Helgesen, Sally, *The Web of Inclusion.* Currency/ Doubleday, New York, NY, 1995.

Hutchins, Robert, *The Conflict of Education in a Democratic Society.* Harper, New York, NY, 1953.

Mathews, David, *Is There a Public for Public Schools?* Kettering Foundation Press, Dayton, OH, 1996.

Odden, Allan and Carolyn Busch, *Financing Schools for High Performance: Strategies for Improving the Use of Educational Resources.* Jossey-Bass Publishers, San Francisco, CA, 1998.

Sarason, Seymour B., *Letters to a Serious Education President.* Corwin Press, Inc., Sage Publications, Inc., Newbury Park, CA, 1990.

Toffler, Alvin and Heidi, *Creating a New Civilization: The Politics of the Third Wave.* Turner Publishing, Inc., Atlanta, GA, 1995.

Tyack, David and Larry Cuban, *Tinkering Toward Utopia: A Century of Public School Reform.* Harvard University Press, Cambridge, MA, 1995.

U.S. Department of Education, National Center for Education Statistics, National Household Education Survey (NHES), 1993.

Walberg, Herbert J., "Productive Teaching and Instruction: Assessing the Knowledge Base," *Phi Delta Kappan*, Feb. 1990.

Lawrence W. Lezotte has long been recognized as the preeminent spokesperson for effective schools research and implementation. As a member of the original team of researchers, Dr. Lezotte, together with Ronald Edmonds and Wilbur Brookover, conducted many of the initial studies of effective schools—schools where all students can achieve academic success.

Effective schools describes a school improvement process that is data-based and data-driven, with effectiveness measured in terms of both quality and equity. These criteria assure a high standard of achievement that does not vary significantly across the subsets of a school's student population.

Since receiving his Ph.D. from Michigan State University in 1969, Dr. Lezotte has worked actively with school districts and practitioners around the nation to implement school improvement programs based on the premises of effective schools research.

Dr. Lezotte was a member of the Michigan State University faculty for 18 years. Currently, he is an educational consultant and researcher at Effective Schools Products, Ltd. in Okemos, Michigan.

As a consultant, writer, and public speaker, Dr. Lezotte continues to touch the lives of thousands of educators and hundreds of thousands of students.

Jo-Ann Cipriano Pepperl holds a journalism degree from Michigan State University, and has worked as a television/radio news reporter, magazine editor, advertising copywriter, and columnist. Her work has appeared in scores of national, regional, and local publications.